"A century after women's suffrage, women still exist under a glass ceiling in American society, which is unfortunately still being scripturally justified within some ecclesial . . . communities. Hertig and her friends . . . help us see that the biblical message is even better news for women than the so-called gospel preached from predominantly male pulpits. Come, Holy Spirit—move afresh upon men and women, young and old, American and Asian—with a new Pentecost!"

—AMOS YONG
Fuller Theological Seminary

"This book is a delightful collection of works that successfully integrates personal stories with scholarly analyses, leading the reader to rediscover new insights from various biblical texts. . . . I strongly recommend *A Biblical Study Guide for Equal Pulpits* as a wonderful tool for pastors, teachers, and seminary students, or simply for anyone who wants to study the Bible in a new way."

—LOIDA I. MARTELL
Lexington Theological Seminary

"I am very grateful for *A Biblical Study Guide for Equal Pulpits*. This collective work by respected practitioner scholars of the Asian American and Latina communities samples homiletics, biblical exegesis, and pulpit ministry *otherwise*. . . . It helps us reposition our biblical readings in the ultimate reality of an equitable God, as supposed to binaries designed to support a hierarchical Eurocentric pulpit."

—OSCAR GARCÍA-JOHNSON
Fuller Theological Seminary

"Hertig's *A Biblical Study for Equal Pulpits* persuasively argues that women of color who are preachers and teachers are the future of the prophetic Christian movement. It's a must-read in our churches, colleges, and faith-rooted justice movements!"

—PETER GOODWIN HELTZEL
Boston University School of Theology

A Biblical Study Guide
for Equal Pulpits

A Biblical Study Guide
for Equal Pulpits

YOUNG LEE HERTIG

Foreword by
EDWIN DAVID APONTE

CASCADE *Books* · Eugene, Oregon

A BIBLICAL STUDY GUIDE FOR EQUAL PULPITS

Cascade Books
An Imprint of Wipf and Stock Publishers
199 W. 8th Ave., Suite 3
Eugene, OR 97401

www.wipfandstock.com

PAPERBACK ISBN: 978-1-6667-1216-2
HARDCOVER ISBN: 978-1-6667-1217-9
EBOOK ISBN: 978-1-6667-1218-6

Cataloguing-in-Publication data:

Names: Hertig, Young Lee, 1954, editor. | Aponte, Edwin David, foreword.

Title: A biblical study guide for equal pulpits / edited by Young Lee Hertig ; foreword by Edwin David Aponte.

Description: Eugene, OR: Cascade Books, 2022. | Includes bibliographical references.

Identifiers: ISBN 978-1-6667-1216-2 (paperback). | ISBN 978-1-6667-1217-9 (hardcover). | ISBN 978-1-6667-1218-6 (ebook).

Subjects: LSCH: Preaching. | Women in Christianity. | Feminist theology. | Women clergy—United States.

Classification: BV4241 B25 2022 (print). | BV4241 (ebook).

VERSION NUMBER 031622

Contents

Foreword

IN THE BOOK OF Proverbs chapter 8 we read these words about Wisdom declaring to the world in multiple ways and in various places, with the hope that people will hear, listen, and possibly change the ways they live their lives (Prov 8:4-6, NRSV):

> To you, O people, I call,
>   and my cry is to all that live.
> ⁵ O simple ones, learn prudence;
>   acquire intelligence, you who lack it.
> ⁶ Hear, for I will speak noble things,
>   and from my lips will come what is right.

Through the honest and important insights of *A Biblical Study Guide for Equal Pulpits* Wisdom is still speaking to us today. This is a historic collaboration in biblical interpretation between Asian American, Asian, and Latinx Christians that is full of fresh insights and practical value for the entire church. Through their individual and shared holistic reexamination of Scripture, we are invited to see the church in more inclusive, expansive, and life-giving ways. Not only do these authors talk about collaboration, but this work demonstrates that they created community and solidarity.

I first became acquainted with the seed of what grew into this important resource through a project that the Louisville Institute funded called Imagining a More Equal Pulpit: Gender Inclusivity and Asian American and Latino/a Churches. That study was directly in line with the mission of the Louisville Institute to bridge church and academy by awarding grants to those who lead and study North American religious institutions, practices, and movements, and thereby promoting scholarship that strengthens church, academy, and society, and contributes ultimately to the flourishing of the church. The Imagining a More Equal Pulpit project explored the ways male control of pulpits in Asian American and Latino/a churches perpetuate a distorted masculinization of Christian faith and life, and thereby contribute to distortions of the message and practice of the gospel. Out of that multiyear project emerged this book, *A Biblical Study Guide for Equal Pulpits*, which directly contributes to the flourishing of the church through both its timely insights and its being a resource for discipleship, calling, leadership, pastoring, and preaching. Here accessible invitations also are invitations to reexamine the Scriptures in creative, imaginative, collaborative, and contextual ways that help unmask cultural traditions that inhibit fuller understandings of the gospel.

As I write these words, the entire world is still in the grips of the global COVID-19 pandemic, which in the context of the United States the multifaceted weight of which has fallen on the poor, and communities of color. Moreover, the pandemic has had global economic impacts that still defy the easy analysis, prediction, and solutions of experts. Concurrent with the virus that already has killed millions throughout the world, the pandemic has brought into the open the need in the United States to directly address issues of racial justice as Blacks and other persons of color continue to be victims of racialized violence and killings perpetrated by White vigilantes and by some police. Once treated by some as the "model minority," Asian Americans experienced increased targeted violence, as some segments of US society blamed Asians for COVID-19 because of the virus's suspected origin in China. In the USA combatting the virus has been politicized so that in some contexts political allegiance has become more important than Christian identity.

In the midst of these overlapping and intersectional realities I was reminded of a visit to Madrid, Spain, that my wife, Laura, and I made in late December 2019, just before there was full global awareness of COVID-19. (In retrospect I suspect that virus was already among us at that time.) In the Lavapiés neighborhood of Madrid, across from subway stop, was a building with two messages emblazoned on two sides. On the windows facing the metro station in giant letters was the phrase "Usted Está Aquí," "You are here." Possibly someone placed that saying there to give people a little smile as they emerged from underground. Around the corner on the same building was a mural that quoted the author and historian Eduardo Galeano (1940–2015), a mural that invited a different type of engagement: "Somos lo que hacemos para cambiar lo que somos," which can be translated "We are what we do in order to change who we are." It seems to me that the two sayings complement each other and serve as an invitation to consider our own contexts. We are here in a world of multiple challenges, including the deadly global virus, a situation of extreme political and cultural divisions, and racial injustices and violence. And these authors identify that one part our contexts is a patriarchy that poses as piety, divides the church, and is a barrier for some siblings in Christ who are called to lead, pastor, and preach. This is where we are, but we also are the ones who can change who we are by the grace of God. We are the ones who in the providence of God are called to this time, to these places, to these specific contexts. We are the ones who are called to do the work of a more equal pulpit. *A Biblical Study Guide for Equal Pulpits* helps us understand where we are and what we should do.

In present contexts that marginalize the voices of women in the church (especially in Asian, Asian American, and Latinx congregations), through these essays we can hear anew the prophetic female voices within Scripture that proclaim wisdom to us. This book calls us to live into the instruction from the apostle Paul found in the Letter to the Romans: "Do not be conformed to this world, but be transformed by the renewing of your minds, so that you may discern what is the will of God—what is good and acceptable and perfect." (12:2 NRSV). Through *A Biblical Study Guide for Equal Pulpits*, we are given guidance in order to avoid being conformed to ways of being and doing that are contrary to the gospel. Like the hearers of Proverbs, who were given the gifts of the woman Wisdom, we are presented the great gifts of the callings and insights of those called by God to proclaim truth, instruction, and knowledge, speaking to church and society insights that we need today. In many parts of the contemporary church there remains a gender gap between those in and not in the pulpit, as too many in ecclesiastical authority follow cultural patterns of male dominance rather than the way of righteousness and the paths of justice. In *A Biblical Study Guide for Equal Pulpits* we find instruction for renewing our minds and doing the will of God, which together help us better understand what all human beings experience. Through engaging with this book, we have the opportunity to expand our imaginations: to rededicate ourselves to God in order to better serve the people of God and the world. In these chapters are trustworthy things for us to hear and embrace, much good counsel, sound judgment, and profound insight for contemporary Christians as we seek to be faithful and effective both as individual disciples and together as faith communities who want to lean into the emerging future. We would all benefit to choose instruction, knowledge, counsel, sound judgment, and insight, from the words of Wisdom as she speaks through *A Biblical Study Guide for Equal Pulpits*.

Edwin David Aponte
Executive Director, Louisville Institute

Contributors

Edwin David Aponte (PhD, Temple University) is Executive Director of the Louisville Institute. As a cultural historian of religions and cultures, Aponte especially explores the intersections of race, ethnicity, and religion, as well as congregational studies and religion and politics. He is the author of *¡Santo! Varieties of Latino/a Spirituality* (2012). He is coeditor of *Handbook of Latina/o Theologies* (2006) and coauthor of *Introducing Latinx Theologies* (2020)—both with Miguel A. De La Torre.

Young Lee Hertig is Executive Director of Innovative Space for Asian American Christianity (ISAAC) and Project Director of PastoraLab. She has authored or edited *The Tao of Asian American Belonging* (2019), *Mirrored Reflections* (Wipf & Stock, 2010), and *Cultural Tug of War* (2001).

Eunny Lee is Associate Professor in the Department of Biblical and Religious Studies at Azusa Pacific University. She has written *The Vitality of Enjoyment in Qohelet's Theological Rhetoric* (2005).

Sophia Magallanes-Tsang is an independent scholar and Assistant Adjunct Professor in the Centro Latino at Fuller Theological Seminary. She is author of *A Pentecostal Commentary on Job* (Wipf & Stock, forthcoming).

Janette H. Ok is Associate Professor of New Testament at Fuller Theological Seminary. She is the author of *Constructing Ethnic Identity in 1 Peter: Who You Are No Longer* (2021), and she is the coeditor of *The New Testament in Color: A Multiethnic Commentary on the New Testament* (forthcoming).

Neal D. Presa is Associate Pastor at Village Community Presbyterian Church (Rancho Santa Fe, California), Research Fellow at the University of the Free State (South Africa), Senior Visiting Professor at Union Theological

Seminary (Philippines), and Visiting Professor at International Theological Seminary (West Covina, California). His books include *Ascension Theology and Habakkuk* (2018), *Liturgical-Missional* (Pickwick Publications, 2016), and *Here Am I, Lord, Send Me* (Resource Publications, 2012).

Kay Higuera Smith is Professor of Biblical and Religious Studies at Azusa Pacific University. She is coeditor of *Evangelical Postcolonial Conversations* (2014).

Gale A. Yee is Nancy W. King Professor of Biblical Studies *emerita* at Episcopal Divinity School. She has authored or edited a number of books, including *Toward an Asian American Biblical Hermeneutics* (Cascade Books, 2021), *The Hebrew Bible: Feminist and Intersectional Perspectives* (2018), *Jewish Feasts and the Gospel of John* (Wipf & Stock, 2007), and *Poor Banished Children of Eve* (2003).

Introduction

Young Lee Hertig

Even as women continue to form the statistical majority in most congregations, the Christian pulpit remains overwhelmingly monopolized by men, thus normalizing and propagating the masculinization of Christianity. Although some mainline denominations have made strides in closing this gender gap, evangelical and independent churches have not followed suit. These churches chose instead to follow the lead of American megachurches and their corresponding complementarian leaders. Under these prxedominantly male-centered pulpits, women clergy are often left facing the unwinnable quandary of either yielding to masculine authority and power or exiting the church all together.

This dilemma is even more pronounced in contemporary ethnic churches such as Asian American and Latino/a congregations. These churches are often reticent to hire women clergy—including women who have come of age in those very churches. Thus, many women of color, both ordained and candidates, are displaced from their ethnic communities and, as a result of this displacement, find themselves serving instead in predominantly Euro-American churches. This trend is unavoidable unless ethnic church pulpits become more equitable. As things stand, the patriarchal culture of these churches will continue to marginalize the voices of women of color, further alienating women leaders as well as women congregants.

It's a sobering realization that in the twenty-first century the gender gap in the pulpit continues to widen. This unbalanced and unjust organizational structure hinders the fullness of the body of Christ. Although gender equality was at the forefront of ecumenical conversations in the 1980s and

1990s, discussions on sexuality and gender identity now largely take center stage in mainline denominations, as an unintended consequence pushing aside issues of gender equality. And while conversations about gender equality on the one hand and gender identity and sexuality on the other need not be mutually exclusive, conversations about gender inequality appear to have waned without resolution. In the meantime, women clergy, both ordained and barred from ordination, who continue to pursue their God-given calls suffer under a cycle of being overworked and underpaid. Despite the church's unwillingness to hire or promote women to lead their congregations, these women still find ways to serve. Unfortunately, this decision too often comes at a high cost to their vocational affirmation, personal well-being, and social standing. If we do not act to remedy this exploitive situation, women clergy will continue to experience the limiting of their sacred gifts and will continue to endure the injustice of unequal access and pay.

We believe the transformation of patriarchal church culture, particularly within ethnic churches, is not feasible unless gender equality is modeled in the pulpit. When voices and representations are overwhelmingly constricted, the fullness of the body of Christ weakens and public witness wanes. Until we turn our full attention to dismantling the obstacles to the fair and equitable ordination and placement of women of color, this experience of wholeness will remain incomplete, and this imbalance will remain harmful to the church's mission. It is the male-gendered pulpit, with its symbolic and discursive position of male *authority over* women, that reinforces male-dominance in the life of the church as well as in the family. *The consequences* of maintaining a male-centric pulpit are enormous in terms of their sociopolitical, economic, and moral impact, injuring the body of Christ in many ways, such as by:

- Losing younger generations of women leaders
- Modeling deep structural power inequality in a culture of blatant disparities
- Undercompensating the work of women clergy
- Increasing violence against women and women's bodies within the church and in the world
- Robbing the body of Christ of the fullness of the gospel
- Silencing the voices of gifted women preachers

- Continuing the masculinization of Christianity, thus imposing upon it a contingent and particular ideology that presents itself as universal

For the reasons above and more, the Asian American and Latina biblical scholars featured in this volume have developed a biblical study guide with the goal of making academic biblical hermeneutical work accessible to the pulpit. In these pages, we have reappropriated a gendered approach to the text, setting aside the male-centric and patriarchy-supporting approaches used in our institutions and instead look at the text through a more equal frame. The work presented in this study guide is based on our "Imagining A More Equal Pulpit" project (funded by the Louisville Institute, with invaluable support from executive director Edwin David Aponte), with the aim of entering into difficult conversations about gender and power in both the Old Testament and the New Testament and generating resources toward transforming the church and restoring the body of Christ.

CHAPTER SUMMARIES

Chapter 1

Kay Higuera Smith's "Two Mothers—Two Promises" takes a perspective-shifting look at two biblical matriarchs, Sarah and Hagar. Higuera Smith invites the reader to consider these women as archetypes of Israel, bearers of divine promises and of Israel's prophetic future. Through highlighting overlooked scripturtal passages, this chapter narrates how Sarah and Hagar are the active recipients of God's divine promises for Israel's prophetic future. This is in contrast to largely passive roles the patriarchs are depicted in. In Abraham's case, it is his wife Sarah, and a foreign slave woman, Hagar, who advance God's promises to Israel. Their active work in delivering divine promises subverts our expected cultural norms. Yet, we often undervalue or ignore their work, even to the point of deriding it from the pulpit as examples of undesirable behavior. But the biblical text shows that it must be through Sarah, and not Abraham alone, that God's promise is fulfilled. *She* is the key figure who ensures Israel's prophetic future. As such, Sarah is the one portrayed as an archetype of Israel, surrounded by mighty empires and called upon to actively engage her many resources. It is Sarah who is the embodiment of the story of the exodus. Higuera Smith goes on to argue that the idea of God's promises being revealed in Sarah and Hagar lines up with the norms of the Hebrew Bible, where there are no essentialized gender

3

differences between men and women. Indeed, women in the Hebrew Bible, as opposed to the ancient Greek worldview, are depicted as institutional sages, and function as generals, strategists, counselors, and prophets.

Chapter 2

Gale A. Yee's "Cast Your Burden on the Lord: Praying the Psalms" elevates the significant but often neglected prayers of lamentation in Psalms. While these psalms are rarely preached from the pulpit, without these laments, we are left only with a "happy face" theology. Without lament, a covenantal relationship becomes a practice of denial, a cover-up of the real feelings and experiences that people confront. Through laments, the voiceless and the powerless can express their hardship by speaking truth to power. In lamenting, the speakers of these psalms invoke the God of justice for restoration of the covenantal relationship with the people of God in the here and now. These prayers (given within this chapter in the inclusive first-person) are understandably gender-neutral and encompass the utterances of men and women alike. Yee looks at these laments through the frame of injustice and social oppression, specifically in the anguish of the victims of domestic violence, who would resonate with the laments depicted in Psalm 55. Psalm 55:20–22, in particular, depict the cycle of domestic violence that alternates between "speech smoother than butter" and "a heart set on war."

Chapter 3

Eunny P. Lee's "Valorous and Wise: Women Who Build Up the House of God" depicts two women, Ruth and the woman of Proverbs 31, as builders of the household. We see that the Hebrew Bible affirms the equal partnership of men and women as they together reflect the image of God. Yet too often women are buried "in between the lines or beneath the lines of Scripture." In the example of Ruth and her mother-in-law, Naomi, they survive and sustain their "house" despite famine, displacement, childlessness, and the loss of their husbands. Furthermore, their survival impacts the larger biblical story, because at stake is the future of the house of David. Indeed, Ruth is placed among the ranks of Israel's matriarchs. It is through this notion of "mother's house," that we see women acting with agency and voice and emerging as "the prominent builders of the house of Israel." In Lee's other example, the woman of Proverbs 31, we see wisdom personified as a woman who is the key component for building houses. Noteworthy is the language regarding "Wisdom's house" (9:1) where Wisdom and God the Creator collaborate in creative activity. While the book of Ruth depicts women as partners with God in building up the house of Israel, the book of Proverbs takes it beyond the private and into the public sphere.

Chapter 4

Sophia Magallanes-Tsang's "Listening for Your voice; Let Me Hear It: The Prophetic Feminine Voice in Songs 8" interprets the Song of Songs as a prophetic female voice based on the *prophetic orthopathos* of Scripture coined by Samuel Solivan. *Prophetic orthopathos* refers to the Holy Spirit's transforming of suffering and despair into hope and wholeness. The female voice of the Song of Songs depicts the church's desire for divine intimacy over two millennia. This interpretation sees the Song of Songs as protest literature, pushing traditional moral boundaries and challenging the power structures of monarchy and patriarchy. Contrary to traditional interpreters, Magallanes-Tsang takes readers beyond the eros of two lovers to the cultural power dynamics between the Shulamite, a woman of color and outsider to the Israelites, and her lover, informing the prophetic dimension of the text. In this prophetic reading, the Song of Songs is seen as a critique of the Solomonic legacy. As the previous chapters demonstrate, so this chapter also highlights the matriarch as a "nesting matriarchy" within the patriarchal culture. God's Spirit continues to speak through those who are being silenced in our churches today as God spoke through the Shulammite's voice.

Chapter 5

Janette H. Ok's "Pulling Up a Seat at the Leader's Table" takes on the often-discussed story of Martha and Mary. However, rather than the usual pitting of one sister against the other, Ok shows both women to be exemplary disciples, each in their unique way. They each embrace Jesus and his mission and act out of love for him. Martha carries the mantle of convention while Mary's unconventional boldness breaks boundaries by pulling up a seat at the table usually reserved for men. In return, Mary receives Jesus' affirmations while Martha is reprimanded by Jesus, though not for her work but for her complaint against Mary. Here, Ok posits that there is a qualitative difference between sitting with Jesus and working for Jesus. Sitting at the male-dominant table may require courage at the beginning, but we can be encouraged by our biblical role models in the journey.

Chapter 6

Young Lee Hertig's "Mordecai and Esther: Intercultural Negotiation of Power Dynamics" shows us another example of women breaking boundaries as outsiders. Here we have Mordecai and Esther making their entries into the Persian palace. Their exemplary collaboration uncovers the unusual twists and turns of navigating palace power structures. Their life in the king's palace unfolds like a Shakespearean drama and results in their saving their people from imminent genocide. Anchored in the spirituality of Purim, Esther courageously risks her life to come before the king without invitation. Next, a series of Queen Esther's banquets not only disarms Haman, who plots genocide against the Jews, but also moves King Xerxes to ultimately reverse Haman's plot. Throughout this process, the strategic partnership between Mordecai and Queen Esther transforms the power structure of the palace. Ample parallels can be found here for Asian American women faith leaders, who are often outsiders to the Asian American pulpit, perpetually facing the "stained glass ceiling." The forging of partnerships with male allies and or coconspirators is crucial in breaking through the barriers to the church's male-dominant pulpits.

Chapter 7

Neal D. Presa's "A Call from a PRI Male Coconspirator" presents an egalitarian hermeneutic lens by dismantling two of the passages most often used against women's full pastoral leadership (1 Cor 14:33–36 and 1 Tim 2:11–14). Drawing from the ancient examples of women as colaborers with the apostle Paul, Presa differentiates what is timeless and spaceless from what are contextual particularities misappropriated today by complementarian theology. We see that the particularities of the Corinthian church are not a prescription for all women. Instead, what matters for Paul is the reality of the risen life of Jesus Christ in the ecclesial community (1 Cor 15:1–2). As with the Corinthian contexts, 1 Tim 1:11–14 also remains contextually particular while ultimately pointing to the divine-human distinction instead of gender distinctions. In place of a problematic complementarian interpretation, we find that the apostle Paul's teaching and admonition can and does apply to both men and women.

1

Two Mothers—Two Promises

KAY HIGUERA SMITH

MANY OF US HAVE learned about the three biblical patriarchs: Abraham, Isaac, and Jacob. We hear their names repeated multiple times in the books of Genesis (50:24), Exodus (2:24; 3:6, 15, 16; 4:5; 6:3; 6:8; 33:1), Leviticus (26:42), Numbers (32:11), Deuteronomy (1:8; 6:10; 9:5, 27; 29:13; 30:20; 34:4), 2 Kings (13:23), and Jeremiah (33:26). The refrain is taken up in the Gospels and in Acts as well (Matt 1:2; 8:11; 22:32; Mark 12:26; Luke 3:34; 13:28; 20:37; Acts 3:13; 7:8, 32). We take for granted that God made a covenant with "Abraham, Isaac, and Jacob." However, as we read the text of Genesis, what we'll find is that the three patriarchs were often passive in ensuring that God's promises were kept. Instead, in each case, it was his wife or even his female slave that rendered certain the divine fulfillment of God's promises.

Let's take a journey through ancient Israel to see the significant roles played by these women in advancing God's promises to Israel. Beginning with the case of Abraham's wife Sarah, we will find that it is her work, along with that of a foreign slave girl, that guarantees the fulfillment of God's promise. These two women are the true active agents in the story of Abram/Abraham.

SARAH, ABRAHAM'S MUSE (GENESIS 11:26—21:21)

Read Genesis 11:26—21:21, then read the following notes and answer the questions in the text boxes.

Sarai and Abram

We first read about Sarah (whose given name is Sarai) in Genesis 11:29 as the wife of Abram (who is later renamed Abraham). Together with Abram's father, Terah, they leave Abram's hometown of Ur of the Chaldeans to travel to the land of Canaan (Gen 11:28, 31). Thereafter, Terah dies during their temporary settlement in the region of Haran (Gen 11:31). It is then that God appears to Abram and makes a promise to him (Gen 12:1–3).

Read the following passage and answer these questions:[1]

Read Genesis 12:1–3

1. To whom does God make the promise?

2. What is the scope of the promise?

3. What action is required for the promise to take effect?

Abram obeys God and sets off for Canaan. He takes with him his nephew Lot, as well as Sarai and "the people whom he had acquired" (Gen 12:5), meaning his slaves and servants.[2] All of these people make up Abram's household. The slaves and servants would be indentured servants, who served their owners and were treated as chattel (property) in the ancient Near East.

---

1. Suggested answers to all the questions are given at the end of the chapter.

2. All Scripture citations are from the New Revised Standard Version. It is recommended to use this version or one that is considered a formal equivalence translation rather than a dynamic equivalence translation.

Indentured Servants in the Hebrew Bible

We often read of indentured servants and slaves in the Hebrew Bible. These servants were subjugated to their masters in all things. In the case of female servants, this included being used sexually (see Gen 16:1–4; 30:1–5, 9–10). Therefore, slavery was especially egregious for women, who were deprived of both sexual and reproductive control over their bodies.

Enslavement was largely permanent, as non-Israelite slaves were considered chattel (property) and were included in the estate, which passed to heirs through inheritance (see Lev 25:46). However, male Israelite slaves could potentially earn their freedom after six years of servitude (see Gen 29:20; 30:26; 31:41; Hos 12:13; Ezek 29:20). This opportunity was unfortunately not given to non-Israelite slaves, nor usually to female Israelite slaves (see Exod 21:2–3; Lev 25:40–42; Deut 15:12; Jer 34:14), but female Israelite slaves had a potential—though narrow—path to freedom. If their new owner deprived them of food, clothing, or conjugal visits, then the female slave could petition for freedom to become an independent woman (see Exod 21:7–11). But even if they earned their freedom, this freedom was complicated by the assumption that they would have been sexually used by their male owners or their sons, thus making marriage difficult, if not impossible, for them. This double bind put emancipated female Israelite slaves in a precarious social and economic position, as neither emancipated nor slave women had the authority to control their own bodies or reproduction.

For these reasons, along with the injustices perpetrated on slaves in general, Israel's prophets disdained the institution of slavery and looked forward to a day when every Israelite servant would be free (see Jer 34:8–11; Ezek 34:27).

THE PROMISE

We return to the story of Abram and Sarai. Upon Abram's arrival at Shechem, which is in the region of Canaan, God appears to him again and gives him a second promise. In this case, the promise is a blessing of land to Abram's offspring (Gen 12:7). Abram builds an altar at Shechem, as well as in the hills east of Bethel (Gen 12:8). He then continues his travels, eventually arriving at the far southern region of the Negev (12:9).

Sojourns in Egypt and Gerar (Gen 12:11—13:1; 20:1–18; 26:1–16)

The first place in which we begin to see the importance of Sarai is in Genesis 12:11—13:1. In this narrative, Abram and his entourage are forced to leave Canaan and journey south to Egypt because of drought. This is the first of three *type scenes*, in which the same event occurs on more than one occasion with the characters and setting slightly changed. The label *type scene* is used because the story recurs three times, twice with Abram and Sarai (Gen 12:11–13:1; 20:1–18) and once with Isaac and his wife, Rebekah (26:1–16). The presence of a type scene generally tells us that something more than meets the eye is at stake. Let's see if we can figure out what it is.

So far, Sarai has not been named as a part of the promise. But it is here, in Egypt, that we begin to recognize that she is an important player—perhaps *the* most important player, in the promise. Read the stories below and answer the following questions:

Read Genesis 12:11—13:1 along with Genesis 20:1–18 and 26:1–16

1. What do the three stories have in common?

2. How are the three stories different?

3. What occurs directly before each story?

4. What role, if any, does God play in each story?

5. In the two stories in chapters 12 and 20, in which Abram and Sarai are the characters, can you find parallels between Sarai's character and the story of the Israelites being forced into slavery in Egypt in Exodus 1:1—13:16? Together, list the parallels.

6. Why might Abram have called Sarai "beautiful in appearance" (Gen 12:11) if she was at the first kidnapping sixty-five years old (Gen 12:4), and in the second kidnapping story ninety years old (Gen 17:17)?

From your study of the three type-scene stories, hopefully you discovered that there are distinct parallels between Sarai and Israel. For one, despite her likely advanced age, Sarai is called "beautiful in appearance." In Genesis 17:17, Abraham (now renamed) laughs at God, who, in giving the covenant to Abraham, mentions again the promised child that must be born to Sarah. Abraham laughs, noting that he is near one hundred, and that Sarai (also renamed Sarah—see Genesis 17:15) is ninety.[3]

In the next chapter, and *before* the second type-scene story, YHWH appears to Abraham to tell him that the birth of the promised child is coming soon. YHWH specifically asks for Sarah to join Abraham as recipient of the promise. God reinforces the importance of Sarah: "No, but your wife Sarah shall bear you a son" (17:19); "But my covenant I will establish with Isaac, whom Sarah shall bear to you" (17:21); "I will surely return to you in due season, and your wife Sarah shall have a son" (18:10); "At the set time, I will return to you, in due season, and Sarah shall have a son" (18:14). Finally, we are told, "The LORD dealt with Sarah as he had said, and the LORD did for Sarah as he had promised" (21:1). It is clear that Sarah is no minor character in the promise. Abraham's faithfulness alone is not sufficient. The child cannot be born merely through Abraham. It must come through Sarah.

Supporting the importance of Sarah for the narrators, we are told in the two type scenes that Sarah was desirable enough for these kings to want to possess her.[4] This should surprise us because we have been told that she is sixty-five in one of the scenes and ninety in the other.[5] We will see that her desirability, despite her age, is an indicator of her symbolic status as an archetype for Israel. In Genesis 18:12, the narrator tells us that Sarah describes herself this way: *"After I have grown old* [lit. "am withered, all worn out"], *and my husband is old, shall I have pleasure?"*

After this self-description, it should also surprise us to hear that when Abraham again travels to another king's realm—in this case the king of Gerar—Abraham is again fearful enough about Sarah's desirability that he tries to pass her off as his sister. As Pharaoh had done, so the king of Gerar "sent and took her" (Gen 20:2). The king's intent must have been sexual because God had to come to him in a dream to warn him against taking such action (vv. 3–7). Could it be simply that Sarah aged extremely well? Or is there another possible reason for her to be presented as so desirable?

---

3. Genesis 17:24 tells us that when Abraham obeyed YHWH and circumcised himself and his household, he was actually ninety-nine years old.

4. We refer to the narrators rather than a single author because the events occurred over many years and were likely passed down through the tradition until finally codified in the book of Genesis. In this sense, it was not a single author but a series of narrators who passed the story down from generation to generation.

5. See Farber, "Is Sarah Old or Young."

The interpretation that her desirability is symbolic of Israel's own sense of its desirability by God and the nations is inspired by the thrice-told type scene. These three narratives tell us that the story must have been widely shared in ancient oral traditions—around firesides and among women while preparing meals. Could it be that Sarah is meant to be a prefigurative image of Israel itself? Could it be that Sarah herself is presented as an Israel figure? Let's look at the parallels.

Sarah	Israel
Taken into Egypt by another	Taken into Egypt by others
Desired by Pharaoh	Desired by Pharaoh to work for him
Freed by the imposition of plagues	Freed by the imposition of plagues
Her freedom resulted in the patriarch being enriched	Their freedom resulted in the patriarch being enriched

The parallels are too much to ignore. This is the first example of what will be a common theme in the stories of Israel's women: a female figure serving as an archetype, or symbolic image, that represents Israel. It is no surprise that Israel's narrators chose women to signify Israel. For Israel was a small, powerless nation—people surrounded by empires with much greater might than their own, who recognized themselves as wise, resourceful, desirable, and competent, despite their weaker status. As Israel's storytellers cast about for an image to archetypally signify their social situation, women made the most sense. Seen as physically inferior in comparison to their male counterparts, who possessed greater physical strength and weaponry, they yet proved to be wise, resourceful, desirable, and competent. This is the depiction of an array of women in the Hebrew Bible.

In this context, Sarah is no throwaway figure. She embodies what will become the people of Israel, just as eventually her grandson Jacob will (Gen 32:28). A central figure in the story of Israel's redemption, she both symbolically represents Israel and ensures that its promises will endure. With this assumption, we can understand the need to present Sarah as so desirable, even at age sixty-five, and again at age ninety. Given that Israel's ancient narrators viewed their own people as desirable among the nations, it makes sense that they would develop oral traditions depicting Sarah and other women as Israel-figures who archetypally represent their nation and their people. Beautiful Sarah, desired among the nations, entrapped and enslaved but ultimately freed by her God, emerges enriched and enlarged by her experience, sent forward to be a blessing to the world. Her story parallels the story of the exodus. Sarah herself is the embodiment of this story.

The reality is that Sarah is essential to the promise. Yet, we often overlook her when we consider the promise made to Abraham. We think of Abraham as the recipient, but as we have seen above, it must be through Sarah, and not Abraham alone, that the promise is fulfilled. *She* is the key figure that ensures Israel's prophetic future.

Did Patriarchy Exist in the Pentateuch?

Something like what we now call patriarchy—a social system in which the rights of the male head of household are enshrined in legal and social codes—may have existed to some extent during the period in which the stories of the patriarchs and matriarchs of Israel were narrated. However, it was a very different social system than what we encounter today in many countries, especially in the West. It was equally a different social system from later patriarchal systems such as the Roman system of *patria potestas* that we encounter in the New Testament. In the period when the Pentateuch was composed, two distinguishing social characteristics influenced gender relations.

1. There is no essentialized gender difference between men and women in the Hebrew Bible. The idea of essentialized gender differences is that femaleness, and, by extension all women, have essential characteristics that are fully distinct from maleness, and, by extension all men. In an essentialized gender hierarchy, women—all women—lack the capacity for the same rational, analytical thought that men possess. Therefore, in order to maintain a harmonious society, its leaders must fix determined roles for each gender that align with their essential natures. This is a common assumption in ancient Greek writings. We see it first with Hesiod. Then we see it with Aristotle, who argues that women lack the capacities to rule, to strategize, and to operate in the public sphere.

Aristotle insists that women have deficiencies in their biological makeup that make it impossible for them to carry out such tasks. Not being privy to what we now know as accurate biological evidence, Aristotle writes from his own rudimentary observations. From them, he concludes that women are the product of deficiencies in the formation of the fetus, while men represent its healthy development. As a result of these fundamentally inaccurate conclusions, Aristotle argues that women's natures require them to obey and to be subservient precisely because, biologically, they lack the rational capacities present in men.

We do not, however, find this notion of essentialized gender differences reflected in how women are portrayed in the Hebrew Bible. Instead, women are often active agents; they often reason better than men; they carry out many of the same tasks as men; they are called upon as institutional sages; and they serve as generals, strategists, counselors, and prophets. To be sure, biblical law was determined on protecting the interests of the male heads of households, but this concern was not predicated on the notion of women lacking any capacity of rationality, decision-making, or leadership. So, though it was indeed the case that there were some divisions of labor, these partitions were not established out of a systemic belief in essentialized gender differences. Instead, gender-specific tasks were largely assigned for pragmatic reasons such as the generally superior physical strength of men or the realities of childbearing (including childbirth) and child-rearing for women.

2. The classic public/private categories of patriarchy developed with the emergence of the urban Greek city-state. However, these categories were not applicable to either the nomadic or agricultural economies operating in the times of the biblical matriarchs and patriarchs. In such economies, a strict distinction between public and private was irrelevant. Nomadic societies, in which people were constantly on the move, did not yield to social organization that assigned exclusive roles to either men or women. We are told, for instance, that Rachel was a shepherd, and shepherding was a task in which men engaged as well. In fact, God is often referred to as a shepherd (Gen 29:6–9; cf. 48:15; 49:24; Num 27:17; 2 Sam 5:2; 7:7). Rachel's tasks as a shepherd would have required her to range abroad with the sheep and to operate outside the physical protections of her male relatives. By the same token, men participated in food preparation and household chores. Genesis 18:7–8 narrates Abraham preparing a meal for his divine guests. Preparing meals, caring for livestock, and producing necessary goods were all carried out by both men and women, and Israel's narrators took this for granted and did not comment on it as notable.

Like nomadic societies, agricultural societies also do not lend themselves to rigid gender role assumptions. Consider the harvest period in agricultural societies. When the harvest comes in, all hands are required to work outside in the fields together, both men and women. We see this exemplified in the book of Ruth. Women in ancient Near Eastern agricultural societies were just as active as men and shared duties in producing the food, clothing, and necessities of life.

Like men, ancient women were managers of households. Today, when we think of households, we imagine the nuclear family. However, in the ancient Near East, a household could encompass hundreds of people, both men and women, over which elite women such as Sarah exercised authority (see Gen 7:1; 26:14; 36:6). Archaeological evidence shows that it was quite common for women to manage and wisely administer such extended households that met all the needs of its extended members as well as the needs of others outside the household.[6] Given that Abraham's household ran into the hundreds, Sarah herself was a prime example of such a competent household manager. There is no indication that she lacked the rational capacities of the men or their leadership ability, nor did she lack in spiritual insight. To be sure, she made at least one decision that seemed questionable. She was the one who suggested to Abram to use Hagar, her own female slave, in order to fulfill the divine promise. We will see, however, that her decision, troublesome as it was, had beneficial results from the perspective of the narrators and ultimately resulted in Hagar's attaining freedom and some prosperity.

Additionally, in the end, it was Sarah who clung to the belief that Isaac, not Hagar's son Ishmael, would be the child of promise (more on Hagar and on Sarai's treatment of her below) while Abraham's desire was that it would be Ishmael (Gen 17:18). Sarah got it right. Abraham got it wrong, consistently resisting that decision, requiring him to be corrected by God on more than one occasion.

What we can conclude from the text is that divisions of labor were based on pragmatic needs such as physical strength or the constraints of childbirth and child-rearing, rather than on essentialized gender role assumptions. The text also tells us that gender hierarchies themselves shifted and transformed in response to the needs of local economies and were not embedded in nature or in some sort of divine economy. These hierarchies themselves were not rigid and essentialized. As Tikva Frymer-Kensky has observed, "Though patriarchy preexisted the Bible, the Bible was not written to construct it."[7]

6. See, for instance, Abigail's authority in 1 Samuel chapter 25. See also 2 Kings chapters 4 and 8.

7. Frymer-Kensky, *Reading the Women of the Bible*, xiv.

> "Though patriarchy preexisted the Bible,
> the Bible was not written to construct it."
> —*Tikva Frymer-Kensky*

Read Genesis 16:1–6A; 17:15—18:15; 21:1–14

1. What evidence do we see in 16:1–6 regarding the nature of the relationship between Sarai and Abram? Who is active and who is passive?

2. In 17:15–22; 18:9–15, what is the significance of Sarah in the interchange between God and Abram/Abraham?

3. In 17:18, does Abraham get it right? What are our narrators trying to tell us here? What would have happened if Abraham's will had been established in the household rather than Sarah's?

4. In 21:9–14, what does God command Abraham to do?

5. How does this align with some more contemporary notions of family hierarchy? Does this indicate a gender hierarchy based on rigid notions of roles for men and women? Does this indicate a gender hierarchy that assumes essential differences in nature between men and women?

SARAH AND HAGAR (GENESIS 16:1-16; 17:18-27; 21:9-21)

Read Genesis 16:1-16; 21:9-21; then read the following notes and answer the questions in the text boxes.

One of the most troubling stories in this cycle is of the relationship between Sarah and her Egyptian slave, Hagar. In this story, Hagar is disadvantaged in three ways: she is an African Egyptian—a foreigner, likely with dark skin; she is a slave; and she is a woman. As a slave, she does not possess reproductive rights over her own body. Moreover, it is clear that Sarah, as her mistress, has internalized the assumptions of her era and sees nothing wrong with using Hagar's body for her own purposes. Because of this troubling narrative, some church traditions will sanction the abuse of Hagar, while also deriding Sarah herself for her role in Hagar's abuse. We hear sermons preached that Sarah, because she is a woman, takes matters into her own hands and gets it wrong. Therefore, it is asserted, it is wrong for any woman to take matters into her own hands. In this construction, Sarah as agent becomes vilified, and thus women's agency in general is warned against.

However, this argument shows at least two blind spots. First, Sarah is far from the only flawed biblical hero who takes matters into their own hands. The Bible is full of such heroes who unwittingly carry out the divine will. One might even call this a motif in the Bible—the unlikely redeemer. Second, we have seen Abraham himself attempt to take matters into his own hands and also get it wrong—at least from the perspective of the narrators of Genesis. The most notable example is in his repeated efforts to advocate for Ishmael as the child of promise.

In Sarah's treatment of Hagar we see that there are no flawless characters in this story. Nevertheless, Sarah's humanity is no different than the humanity of the various male characters in Israel's narratives, who are flawed and also make mistakes, but who nevertheless carry out God's promises.

A careful reading of the Hagar cycle reveals some striking observations about how gender was conceived in the Genesis tradition. First, there is a puzzling story that appears to sanction abuse of slaves by their masters. In 16:6, Sarai abuses Hagar, causing Hagar to run away. What is puzzling is that the angel of the Lord speaks to Hagar and tells her, "Return to your mistress and submit to her" (v. 9). Why would the angel tell Hagar to return to an abusive situation and submit to it? Does this reflect some sort of affirmation of abuse by a slaveholder? What other possible reasons might there be for this divine command? We can only speculate. On one hand, it may have been a command to ensure Hagar's survival. Pregnant, she likely would have died in the wilderness. To return to Sarai, despite the abuse, likely meant survival. This interpretation is strengthened by the events of Genesis 21:9–21, where Hagar faces a similar situation but with a different outcome. There, instead of Hagar running away, Sarah instructs Abraham to send her away, which he does. In this case, however, Ishmael is older and stronger, and Hagar survives and is finally able to achieve independence and to raise her son as a free and autonomous woman.

A second possible reason for the story of abuse is to highlight Hagar as another woman who stands as an archetype for Israel. Hagar's story—of an Egyptian enslaved by a foreign people, with no control over her own body or fate, used and abused by her masters—may have been an ironic comfort to Israelites, who would see the parallels in their enslavement to, ironically, the Egyptians. They also would also have been used and abused by their masters. They also would have had no control over their own bodies or fates, and their women would have been vulnerable to sexual assault and unwanted child-rearing. We see that, like Israel, Hagar will ultimately receive unusual blessings from God. The command for her to accept her fate may be a command that the narrators of Genesis found comforting to their own people as a way to help them temporarily accept their fate until redemption and blessing could come.

Note also that in the earlier story, in which Hagar runs away and ultimately returns (Gen 16), the angel of the Lord gives Hagar, the slave woman, a singular honor given to no other woman in Israel's narratives (vv. 6–14). The angel comforts Hagar and gives her a divine promise of descendants (v. 10). This is not just any promise. It is the only case in the Bible in which God gives a promise of descendants directly to a woman. In this, then, the biblical narrators, focused as they are on Isaac's story and despite their own interests, record a unique and unparalleled promise to Hagar, a foreign woman, likely with darker skin, likely oppressed because of her class, and sexually used as a slave—a woman who would reside on the lowest rungs of the social ladder in her society. Despite the harsh treatment she receives in the narrative, she is renowned and singled out for this unique honor.

Second, it is to her, and not Abram, to whom the angel discloses what the child's name is to be (16:11). After she returns from this encounter, it must be Hagar who instructs Abram what to name the child, because soon thereafter, when the child is born, we are told, "And Abram named his son, whom Hagar bore, Ishmael" (v. 15). We have the surprising case here in which the slave woman, purportedly powerless and voiceless, instructs the master what to name the child, and he follows her directive.

Finally, Hagar is no passive victim. Upon receiving the divine promise, she again shows initiative and courage. She is the first person in the Hebrew Bible to name God. "You are El-Roi," she asserts, a name translated as "God of Vision," or "God Who Sees Me" (v. 13). This is a courageous and audacious act, which memorializes Hagar in Israel's history. Despite her state of subjugation, the text ensures that Hagar will be honored throughout Israel's history. To be sure, Hagar is abused cruelly by both Sarah and Abraham, yet she emerges a free and independent woman, powerful and blessed with unique divine favor. In this sense, Hagar again is an archetype for God's people.

After Hagar has run away and returned at the angel's urging, the story shifts back to Sarai. Here, we see Sarai again taking the initiative and instructing Abram in how to proceed, followed by Abram's acquiescence and obedience. The stereotype of the male head of household who makes all the decisions, and the obedient, passive wife, does not pertain here. We already saw Sarai commanding Abram to impregnate her slave in 16:2, with the response that "Abram listened to the voice of Sarai." The word "listened" in the Hebrew is a form of the well-known verb, *lishmoa*, which means to listen and obey, as in the call to Israel in Deuteronomy 6:4, "Hear (*shma*) O Israel, the LORD is our God, the LORD alone." Thus, another way to translate 16:2, would be, "Abraham listened to and obeyed the voice of Sarai."

This is not the only time that Sarai commands and Abram obeys. These interactions appear commonplace and unsurprising to our narrators. We are told in chapter 21 of Genesis that Sarah finally conceives and bears her son, Isaac, the child of promise. When Isaac is weaned, we are told that Sarah sees Ishmael, Hagar's son, "playing with her son" (v. 9). The Hebrew word there, *metzakheq*, has a range of meaning, from simply "playing with," as the NRSV translates it, to "mocking," "making fun of," or "amusing himself with," which may make more sense in the context (compare Gen 39:14, 17; Judg 16:25). As a result, Sarah again gives Abraham a command, telling him to "cast out the slave woman with her son" (Gen 21:10). Abraham, understandably, does not want to cast out either Hagar or his own son, but, for a second time, God tells Abraham to listen and to follow his wife's instructions: "Whatever Sarah says to you, do as she tells you" (v. 12). That word "do" again translates the Hebrew word *shma*—listen *and obey!* Here again, we see no evidence for a gender hierarchy that forbids a man from following the commands or requests of his wife. Just the opposite: God is the one commanding Abraham to obey his wife. Moreover, it is necessary for God to command Abraham to obey Sarah because Abraham's inclinations are not in accordance with how our narrators depict God's promise. Instead, it is Sarah who is presented as truly understanding how to enact the divine promise.

But this understanding yields a harsh response. Abraham sends Hagar and his own son into a cruel and punishing wilderness. Hagar and Ishmael wander until their water runs out. Hagar, not wishing to witness her own child's death, leaves Ishmael under a tree and cries out in grief (Gen 21:16). It appears that Ishmael also cries out (v. 17). What occurs next consummates the divine vindication of Hagar and Ishmael that began in chapter

16. First, God "called to Hagar from heaven" (v. 17), telling her that God had heard the boy's voice. God speaks to her directly, repeating the promise that the angel had given to her in 16:10–12. Hagar, a woman thrice repressed and horribly robbed of her dignity, is a woman who stands tall and speaks one-on-one with YHWH. Second, Hagar becomes a free woman. God lifts her up, along with the boy, shows them water, and establishes them to the point where Hagar has the resources ultimately to send to her home country, Egypt, to find Ishmael a wife. Her vindication is complete, and her humiliation has been replaced with dignity, honor, and status in her new community.

Read Genesis 16:1–16; 21:9–21

1. It was a common practice among elite women in the ancient Near East to have their slave women bear children on their behalf if they could not produce children themselves. How do we distinguish between practices that are recorded as normative in the Bible and practices that are presented as models for behavior?

2. In Genesis 16:4, we are told that Hagar "looked with contempt on her mistress" once she had conceived. What does this tell us about how status was achieved in the ancient Near East? Can Hagar's contemptuous treatment of Sarai be read as a critique of a system that valued women solely based on their ability to produce offspring? If so, in what way?

3. In Genesis 16:6, we read that Sarah abused Hagar, resulting in Hagar running away for a period of time. Historically, Christian preachers have used this narrative to urge female victims of abuse, whether the abuse is emotional, physical, or sexual, to return to their abusers. Is that the message of this story? Can you suggest other messages in addition to the one given in the study materials above?

4. As we review all the stories in the Sarai/Sarah, Hagar, and Abram/Abraham cycle, where is the focus? Is it on Abram/Abraham, Sarai/Sarah, or Hagar? Who is active in the stories and who is passive? Who takes initiative and who follows directions?

5. If the focus is on the women, why have we been trained to focus our gaze so intently on Abram/Abraham?

6. What are the implications for us today in these stories—especially for Asian, Asian American, Pacific Islander, and Latina women?

RESPONSES TO STUDY SESSION QUESTIONS

Read Genesis 12:1-3

1. To whom does God make the promise?

ANSWER: To Abram

2. What is the scope of the promise?

ANSWER: "I will make of you a great nation, I will bless you, and make your name great, so that you will be a blessing; I will bless those who bless you, and the one who curses you I will curse; and in you all the families of the earth shall be blessed" (Gen 12:2–3).

3. What action is required for the promise to take effect?

ANSWER: "Go from your country and your kindred and your father's house to the land that I will show you" (Gen 12:1 NRSV).

Read Genesis 12:11—13:1 along with Genesis 20:1-18 and 26:1-16

1. What do the three stories have in common?

ANSWER: A patriarch goes to a foreign land, passes his wife off as his sister, is found out, and returns to Canaan with greater wealth.

2. How are the three stories different?

ANSWER: Isaac/Rebekah in chapter 26; Egypt in chapter 12; Gerar in chapters 20 and 26. In chapter 20, Abram uses the excuse that Sarai is indeed his sister.

3. What occurs directly before each story?

ANSWER: God has made a promise to the patriarch.

4. What role, if any, does God play in each story?

ANSWER: In chapter 12, God afflicts Pharaoh and his house with a plague, which causes Pharaoh to realize he has been deceived; in chapter 20, God appears in a dream to Abimelech and orders him to return Sarai under the threat of death; none in the Isaac/Rebekah scene, but God is the one who commands Isaac to stay in Gerar and promises blessings if he does (26:2–5). Ultimately, Isaac is indeed blessed (26:12–14) and Rebekah is spared from any sexual exploitation, unlike Sarai in 12:15.

5. In the two stories in chapters 12 and 20, which narrate the story with Abram and Sarai, can you find parallels between Sarai's character and the story of the Israelites being forced into slavery in Egypt in Exodus 1:1—13:16? Together, list the parallels.

ANSWER: Sarai is forced to live in Egypt; she has no control over her own body; she is beautiful (like Israel); Pharaoh is afflicted with plagues because he brought her into his home (12:15); Abraham is enriched even more than before as a result of the experience (12:16; 13:2).

6. Why might Abram have called Sarai "beautiful in appearance" (Gen 12:11) if she was at the first kidnapping sixty-five years old (see Gen 12:4; 17:17) and in the second kidnapping story, ninety years old (Gen 17:17)?

ANSWER: She symbolized Israel.

Read Genesis 16:1–16; 21:9–21

1. It was a common practice among elite women in the ancient Near East to have their slave women bear children on their behalf if they could not produce children themselves. How do we distinguish between practices that are recorded as normative in the Bible and practices that are presented as models for behavior?

ANSWER: We read the entire Bible to ensure understanding of the norms that the Bible consistently puts forward. Recording an act does not necessarily amount to an affirmation of its moral value. This principle can also be applied to various systems of patriarchy or gender hierarchy. The Bible assumes gender hierarchy in many cases, but it does not advance it as a moral imperative.

2. In Genesis 16:4, we are told that Hagar "looked with contempt on her mistress" once she had conceived. What does this tell us about how status was achieved in the ancient Near East? Can Hagar's contemptuous treatment of Sarai be read as a critique of a system that valued women solely based on their ability to produce offspring? If so, in what way?

ANSWER: It tells us that an elite woman without children could lose status, and that a slave and a foreigner could gain status as the mother of the householder's child. It can be read as a critique because such a system pits the victims of the system against each other. Sarai is a victim because she is childless through no fault of her own. Hagar is a victim because she is forced into a sexual act with her mistress's husband without her consent. The real problem is with the system itself, which victimizes both women.

3. In Genesis 16:6, we read that Sarah abused Hagar, resulting in Hagar running away for a period of time. Historically, Christian preachers have used this narrative to urge female victims of abuse, whether the abuse is emotional, physical, or sexual, to return to their abusers. Is that the message of this story? Can you suggest other messages in addition to the one given in the study materials above?

ANSWER: It may not have been prescriptive; that is, prescribing behavior. It may have been descriptive alone and thus not appropriate for modeling future behavior. Given the overwhelming concern for the marginalized and suffering in the Bible, such an interpretation would require ignoring large sections of the moral instruction found within the Hebrew Scriptures.

4. As we review all the stories in the Sarai/Sarah, Hagar, and Abram/Abraham cycle, where is the focus? Is it on Abram/Abraham, Sarai/Sarah, or Hagar? Who is active in the stories and who is passive? Who takes initiative and who follows directions?

ANSWER: The women are the active agents and the ones who take initiative. God speaks to Hagar just as God speaks to Abram/Abraham. Abram/Abraham is mostly passive.

5. If the focus is on the women, why have we been trained to focus our gaze so intently on Abram/Abraham?

> **ANSWER:** We have been trained to read Scripture through an *andro-centric* (*andro* = male + *centric*) lens. Our eyes lead us to read what we expect, which is that the story centers on Abram/Abraham. A careful reading, however, shows us that in most of the narratives, the women, not Abram/Abraham, are the active agents. This indicates that the women may be even more important than Abram/Abraham in ensuring that the divine promises are carried out.
>
> 6. What are the implications for us today in these stories—especially for Asian, Asian American, Pacific Islander, and Latina women?
>
> **ANSWER:** Free Response. Some suggestions: Implications of these stories include that many gender hierarchies today do not pay sufficient attention to the various forms of patriarchy that shift over time; that they are more dependent upon Aristotle than upon the biblical tradition; that our androcentric tradition, in training our gaze to focus on the male characters, has impoverished us by cloaking the important stories of women enshrined in the pages of the Hebrew Scriptures. When read closely and carefully, the stories of Hagar, Sarah, and Abraham demonstrate that the gender hierarchies that we may have grown up with are culturally contingent and thus not divinely ordained.

BIBLIOGRAPHY

Bellis, Alice Ogden. *Helpmates, Harlots, and Heroes: Women's Stories in the Hebrew Bible.* 2nd ed. Louisville: Westminster John Knox, 2007.

Brenner, Athalya, et al., eds. *Genesis.* Texts@Contexts. Minneapolis: Fortress, 2010.

Day, Peggy L., ed. *Gender and Difference in Ancient Israel.* Minneapolis: Fortress, 1989.

Farber, Zev. "Is Sarah Old or Young When Kidnapped by Abimelech?" *TheTorah.com/.* 2014. https://thetorah.com/article/is-sarah-old-or-young-when-kidnapped-by-abimelech/.

Frymer-Kensky, Tikva. "The Ideology of Gender in the Bible and the Ancient Near East." *Studies in Bible and Feminist Criticism* (2006) 185–93.

———. *Reading the Women of the Bible: A New Interpretation of Their Stories.* New York: Schocken, 2004.

Jacobs, Mignon. *Gender, Power, and Persuasion: The Genesis Narratives and Contemporary Portraits.* Grand Rapids: Baker Academic, 2007.

Kwok, Pui-Lan, ed. *Hope Abundant: Third World and Indigenous Women's Theology.* Maryknoll, NY: Orbis, 2010.

Moss, Candida R., and Joel S. Baden. *Reconceiving Infertility: Biblical Perspectives on Procreation and Childlessness.* Princeton: Princeton University Press, 2015.

Schneider, Tammi J. *Mothers of Promise: Women in the Book of Genesis.* Grand Rapids: Baker Academic, 2008.

2

Cast Your Burden on the Lord
Praying the Psalms

GALE A. YEE

MY PERSONAL CONNECTION TO the Psalms begins in my childhood and continues on to today. As a former Roman Catholic (now Episcopalian), I was born into a religious tradition that revered and prayed the psalms. During the rigors of my PhD, it was listening to the psalms in Gregorian chant that got me through. When I taught at seminary, I would begin my days with students at morning prayer where the Psalms were beautifully sung. And now, when chanting the Psalms at my Sunday Eucharist, I am spiritually uplifted. The Psalms continue to be foundational in male and female monastic communities where prayer is their primary vocation. Here, the psalms are distributed in a structured prayer life so that all 150 psalms are sung once a week.

For over a thousand years, Jews and Christians have seen their lives expressed in the Psalms, which have provided a biblical voice for the many ways they have experienced their "up and down" relationships with God. In Jewish Bibles, the book of Psalms is the first book of the Writings, the third section of the Jewish canon. In Christian Bibles, it is one of the poetical books, following the book of Job.

In this way, they are different from the stories of the Bible. They are not prose pieces, but ancient poems.

As Israelite poetry, the basic feature of the psalms is parallelism, in which an author repeats an idea in paired lines. Another common feature of Israelite poetry is the use of metaphor and figurative language. We see both of these techniques in Psalm 18, where Death is presented in paired lines and metaphorically described as cords and snares that entangle and trap the psalmist.

For example:

> The cords of death encompassed me
>> The torrents of perdition assailed me;
> The cords of Sheol entangled me;
>> The snares of death confronted me. (Ps 18:4–5)

In Psalm 22, we again see the psalmist describe her distress in parallel lines of vivid imagery:

> I am poured out like water,
>> And all my bones are out of joint;
> My heart is like wax;
>> It is melted within my breast;
> My mouth is dried up like a potsherd,
>> And my tongue sticks to my jaws;
> You lay me in the dust of death. (Ps 22:14–15)

Biblical scholars have determined two basic categories of psalms in the book of Psalms: prayers of lament in time of need and songs of praise to God. When we think about it, lament and praise are most often the two ways that we pray to God today: asking God to do something for us and then thanking God when it happens. In many respects, the emotions expressed in the psalms are very familiar to us: they range from sadness, despair, loss, anger, and rage to hope, joy, thanksgiving, and exultation. One psalm can contain several of these sentiments, sometimes in seemingly contradictory combinations. Consider for example Psalm 13, which begins with a statement of pain, sorrow, and victimization by an enemy:

> How long, O LORD? Will you forget me forever?
>> How long with you hide your face from me?
> How long must I bear pain in my soul?
>> And have sorrow in my heart all day long?
> How long shall my enemy be exalted over me? (13:1–2)[1]

---

1. All Scripture passages are from the NRSV.

The psalmist ponders the unimaginable: to be forgotten by God while suffering pain and anguish. Although this psalm and others like it are typically designated as "laments," they are more accurately described as complaints to God, trying to provoke God to some sort of action. We see this in the psalmist's demand:

> . Consider and answer me, O LORD my God!
>   Give light to my eyes, or I will sleep the sleep of death,
> And my enemy will say, "I have prevailed";
>   And my foes will rejoice because I am shaken. (13:3–4)

We usually do not pray in imperatives, commanding God to do something. But these commands directed at God are all over the psalms when one reads them carefully.[2] They express needs of the petitioner that are deeply felt, and then astonishingly move from the psalmist's pain and victimization to a confession of trust in God's steadfast love. His heart rejoices in God's salvation and sings God's praises (vv. 5–6).

Here we can pause and consider the conventional assumption of the psalmist's male gender. While the psalmist's gender is understood to be male in the NRSV due to the superscription at the beginning of the psalm attributing authorship to king David, these superscriptions were secondary additions added over the centuries. But if we bracket the superscription, we can easily imagine women along with men over the centuries reading their own experiences of pain and sorrow into the psalm and then moving toward a confidence in God's steadfast love which will overcome them.

The psalmist's use of the first-person voice is a key feature that permits both male and female readers to read their experiences into the biblical text. The speaker of the psalm is usually an "I" who addresses God intimately as a "You." One example of the "I" comes from Psalm 6, where the psalmist petitions while in the grip of pain:

> I am weary with my moaning;
>   every night I flood my bed with tears;
> I drench my couch with my weeping.
>   My eyes waste away because of grief;
>   they grow weak because of all my foes. (Ps 6:6–7)

Although the superscription again attributes this psalm to David, the familiar experience of going to bed in tears will resonate with both men and

---

2. Cf. "Rouse yourself! Why do you sleep, O Lord? Awake, do not cast us off forever" (Ps 44:23). See also Pss 6:6 and 35:1–3, 22–24.

women. Both genders will be able to identify with the psalm's "I" in the throes of agony.

Similarly, Psalm 30 shows up an "I" experiencing joy, having been touched by God, who had drawn the psalmist up from the pit:

> You have turned my mourning into dancing;
>> You have taken off my sackcloth and clothed me with joy.
> So that my soul may praise you and not be silent.
>> O Lord my God, I will give thanks to you forever. (Ps 30:11–12)

In both of the examples above, the psalms express an I/Thou relationship with God in which both male and female readers can find a voice for their particular emotions and feelings, whether sad or happy, angry or content, painful or joyful.

As we have seen, the psalmist makes imperative commands of God. Because their I/Thou relationship with God is *covenantal*, the authors of these lament psalms dare to demand that God answer them. To understand this, we need to begin with the momentous event of God's covenant with Israel on Mount Sinai in the book of Exodus. Here, God does not simply tell Moses to tell Pharaoh, "Let my people go," just to free them from slavery. More importantly, it is to bring them into the wilderness to enter into an intimate covenantal relationship with the God-who-saves (cf. Exod 7:16; 8:1). In such a relationship, there are significant duties and responsibilities on both parties. If one is faithful to this covenant, he or she is able to call upon God and demand answers to their prayers.

However, we must regard with a critical eye the psalmist's demands of God to enact violence against enemies. For example, the song of those lamenting their cruel deportation from Jerusalem to a foreign land begins thus:

> By the rivers of Babylon—
>> there we sat and there we wept
> when we remembered Zion. (Ps 137:1)

The popularity of Psalm 137 is seen in the number of its musical iterations on its theme of exile.[3] However, none of the renditions end with the revenge scenario of the psalm against their Babylonian captors, in which their babies will be dashed upon the rocks:

---

3. Boney M, "Rivers of Babylon"; The Melodians, "Rivers Of Babylon"; Ronstadt, "Rivers of Babylon."

> O daughter Babylon, you devastator!
>   Happy shall they be who pay you back
> what you have done to us!
>   Happy shall they be who take your little ones
> and dash them against the rock! (Ps 137:8–9)

Nothing but this horrible image communicates more clearly the visceral feelings of anger, rage, and despair that the exiles feel in their captivity and at their captors. They want in their humiliated and captive state for the babies of Babylon to be dashed against the rocks of the Euphrates.

In Psalm 58, the psalmist begs God to break the teeth and tear out the fangs from his enemies' mouths (58:6). These merciless sentiments continue in the following images:

> Let my enemies be like the slug
>   that dissolves into slime.
> Like an aborted fetus
>   that never sees the light of day. (58:8)

> The righteous will rejoice
>   when they see vengeance done;
> they will bathe their feet
>   in the blood of the wicked. (58:10)

How should we feel when these imprecatory (cursing) psalms call upon God to harm or destroy enemies so savagely?

In order to understand such images, we must understand the genre of the laments in which these images are situated. As I mentioned before, laments are better described as complaints to God, protesting the circumstances—not by whining or grumbling but with outbursts springing from very deep emotions, often anger. Furthermore, laments are complaining to God *in faith*. This might seem to be a contradictory: If you complain about your situation, you are not being faithful. However, asking, insisting, and demanding why from God should be an integral part of our faith, perhaps even carrying this emotion-filled why to bid God wreak havoc upon our enemies, as we have it in the laments.

Cursing, calling down wrath upon those who have afflicted us, is not an acceptable part of our culture. The occasional expletive that might slip from our mouths is nowhere near the long lists of curses in the Bible. This is one of the big reasons why the cursing psalms are very troubling in our congregations. But we must remember that even though cursing and calling down violence on our oppressor is an act of performative speech, it is *not* performative action. The psalm leaves the action to God's very self. It resolves our strong emotions by putting us in the context of God's saving power. In the laments we do not conceal, hide, or repress our pain. We speak the truth of our suffering, recognizing that our rage and anger is powerless by itself to change things in the world. In the laments, we acknowledge that we are helpless and overwhelmed in the face of injustice. In the laments, we acknowledge God's power and God's justice and ask God to act on our behalf.

You probably have never heard these troubling images or imprecatory psalms in our worship services. The reason is that they are often excised from our lectionary readings[4] and hymns. Ivan Kaufman, a well-known scholar of the Psalms, examines the Roman Catholic lectionary, the Presbyterian lectionary, the Book of Common Prayer, the Revised Common Lectionary, and lectionaries in the Church of England and of Canada. He reveals how each of these lectionaries excludes the lament psalms or edits them to make them more palatable. Kaufman describes this absence of the lament as being "undercut by joy."[5] By eliminating these deep feelings in the laments from our prayer life, our covenantal relationship with God becomes a one-sided occasion to celebrate joy and well-being. The petitioner becomes either voiceless or limited to words only of praise. Without these laments, we are left only with a "happy face" theology, what my students call an "emoji" theology. We lose touch with the *real* world. The covenantal relationship without lament ultimately becomes a practice of denial, a cover-up of our *real* feelings, wherein our religious services become mute and silenced. Without the laments, how can we raise legitimate questions of social and economic justice? Without the laments, how can we speak truth to power if on the one hand we are voiceless, and on the other the only thing we can express is joy and praise?

The laments insist that things are not right in the present covenantal relationship. Life is not what it was promised to be. The laments insist that things need not stay this way, that they can be changed. The laments bring to the fore a personal grievance against an unjust system, a wrong that needs to be rectified. The laments insist we will not accept this intolerable situation, and, most importantly, that it is the obligation of the God-who-saves

---

4. Lectionaries are the books that contain a list of the scriptural readings for church services in the liturgical year.

5. Kaufman, "Undercut by Joy."

to change them. They mobilize God, who saved in the past, to respond and fulfill his responsibilities in the covenantal relationship here and now.[6]

It should be clear that we continue to need the laments. We need them to allow the victim to speak truth to power, before God, before the community, and before our "enemies." Through the laments we name not only injustice but also its perpetrators. (You will notice in the Psalms that the "enemies" are deliberately vague and ambiguous so as to cover all sorts of "enemies.") Beyond naming injustice, laments pray for and pursue justice. Laments redistribute and rebalance power between the parties of the covenant, by demanding that the God-who-saves keep his part of the covenant. The petitioner is not silenced but taken seriously. She is empowered to bring her crises and troubles before God and to demand that God "get off his butt."

With the laments, we have a more complete prayer. Within the complaints of many laments aspects of praise and thanksgiving are often embedded. For example, after lamenting God's long apparent absence, the petitioner of Psalm 13 declares her trust in God's steadfast love and will sing to the Lord for dealing bountifully with her (13:5–6). It is the painful experiences of life that provide a context for our praise of God, who has saved in the past and will deliver us in the future.

Let us apply what we have learned about laments in an exercise in the interpretative possibilities in reading the Psalms. We noted that the psalmist's convention of using the first-person viewpoint allows for both men and women to read themselves into a psalm. Similarly, the exact identity of the "enemy" in the Psalms is purposefully elusive so that any number and types of adversaries can be construed in a psalm. Because the first-person voice is gender-neutral in its utterance, let us relate the lament to specific traumatic experiences of women. Let us assume, for example, that the petitioner of Psalm 55 is a "she," a victim of domestic violence by her husband.[7] From the outset, the woman's plea for help is directed to God's very self, demanding a response from the deity:

> Give ear to my prayer, O God;
> Do not hide yourself from my supplication.

6. Brueggemann, "The Costly Loss of Lament."
7. Cf. Bail, "'O God, Hear My Prayer.'"

> Attend to me, and answer me;
>> I am troubled in my complaint. (Ps 55:1–2)

Expecting another round of her husband's abuse, she is terrified:

> My heart is in anguish within me,
>> The terrors of death have fallen upon me.
> Fear and trembling come upon me,
>> And horror overwhelms me. (55:4–5)

She wishes an escape from his blows:

> Oh that I had wings like a dove!
>> I would fly away and be at rest;
> Truly, I would flee far away:
>> I would lodge in the wilderness;
>> I would hurry to find a shelter for myself
> From the raging wind and tempest. (55:5–8)

Having no place to go in the home itself, she imagines herself as a dove flying far away. Within the context of her story, one could conceivably assume the "shelter" referred to here as a women's domestic-violence shelter.

Reflecting on her desperate situation, the woman asserts that she could even bear the taunts of her enemies and hide from those who disrespect her:

> It is not enemies who taunt me—
>> I could bear that;
> It is not adversaries who deal insolently with me—
>> I could hide from them. (55:12)

However, she is powerless before the taunts and abuse from the husband, the cause of her misery. She accuses him directly:

> But it is you, my equal,
>> My companion, my familiar friend,
> With whom I kept pleasant company;
>> We walked in the house of God with the throng. (55:13–14)

The one who should have been her equal, her companion, her intimate friend, whom she once trusted, and with whom she once shared a life, is now addressed as "you," the perpetrator of her afflictions.

> My companion laid hands on a friend,
>> And violated a covenant with me. (55:20)

In the context of domestic violence, one can read Psalm 55:20 as a describing a husband violating his marital covenant by his abuse of his wife. One who should have been her "companion" now "laid hands on" or attacked one who should be his "friend."

One of the most insidious aspects in the cycle of domestic violence is the abuser's regret of his abuse. After inflicting violence upon his wife, the husband tries to seduce her back "with speech smoother than butter, with words softer than oil." Studies have revealed that women remain in abusive relationships because periods of ill-treatment are followed by intervals of remorse, kindness, and generosity. Unfortunately, the cycle of violence begins again:

> With speech smoother than butter,
>> But with a heart set on war;
> With words that were softer than oil,
>> But in fact, were drawn swords. (55:20–21)

Just as one must acknowledge that domestic violence is a cycle, moving in flux from abuse to kindness to abuse again, one cannot read Psalm 55 in a linear way from crisis to resolution. After indicting her husband, who should have been her intimate friend but is the perpetrator of her abuse (55:13–14), the woman unleashes her bitter imprecation against her enemies, while calling upon God to deliver her from her toxic position:

> Let death come upon them;
>> Let them go down alive to Sheol;
> For evil is in their homes and in their hearts.
>> But I call upon God,
> And the LORD will save me.
>> Evening and morning and at noon
> I utter my complaint and moan,
>> And he will hear my voice.
> He will redeem me unharmed
>> From the battle that I wage,
> For many are arrayed against me.
>> God, who is enthroned from of old
> Will hear, and will humble them—
>> Because they do not change,
> And do not fear God. (55:15–19)

Besides her abusive husband, there are other "enemies" that the woman accuses and curses:

> Confuse, O Lord, confound their speech;
>> For I see violence and strife in the city.
> Day and night they go around it
>> On its walls,
> And iniquity and trouble are within it;
>> Ruin is in its midst;
> Oppression and fraud
>> Do not depart from its marketplace. (55:2, 9–11)

Within a context of domestic abuse, the reader can imagine an urban setting where "violence and strife," such as harassment and rape against women, are condoned (Ps 55:9). One can visualize the enemies as police who ignore her complaints; neighbors who turn a blind eye; and her own family, who want her to keep silent.

There is an abrupt change in voice from the "I" of the woman to a voice that enjoins the woman to

> Cast your burden on the LORD
>> and he will sustain you;
> He will never permit
>> The righteous to be moved. (55:22)

Some read this verse as a sarcastic continuation of the husband's "speech smoother than butter and words softer than oil." However, the openness of the narrative permits another voice to enter scene, perhaps that of a friend, perhaps that of a clergy person, who exhorts the wife to throw herself upon God's divine protection.

And the woman listens to this voice. She casts her burden onto the Lord, and summons the courage to call upon God in her despair to deal with her enemies:

> But you, O God, will cast them down
>> Into the lowest pit;
> The bloodthirsty and treacherous
>> Shall not live out half their days. (55:23a–b)

In the allusions to the "lowest pit," she prays that God will mete out the worst punishment for these offenders, namely, death itself. This prayer refers back to her wish for her enemies in 55:15:

> Let death come upon them;
>> Let them go down alive to Sheol;
> For evil is in their homes
>> And in their hearts.

Ultimately, whatever destination or fate may befall her enemies through God's intervention, the coda of her prayer puts this in God's hands: "I will trust in you" (55:23c). In the intimate covenantal relationship with God, she recognizes and acknowledges God as her advocate and protector.

CONCLUSION

The book of Psalms is a time-tested spiritual resource, used over millennia by millions of Christians and Jews in worship and prayer all over the world. The psalms differ from the narrative portions of the Bible as they are prayers written as poetry that were sung and prayed by the ancient Israelites in their temple, synagogues, and households. Although many of the psalms are attributed to King David and others, scholars agree that these attributions are doubtful. Rather, the authors of these psalms were primarily anonymous believers. As individuals or in a group at different historical periods, they prayed fervently to their God, their prayers encapsulated in poetic verse.

Psalms are generally of two types. The first are the songs or hymns of praise. Some of these hymns praise God's creation (Pss 8; 33; 104) or God's steadfast love for the people (Pss 103; 117) or God's saving power (Pss 111; 146). Many psalms thank God for deliverance from enemies (Ps 30) and God's wondrous deeds (Ps 75).

The second and most common psalm type is the lament or complaint, in which the petitioner approaches God with a request. Their requests cover a wide range of human problems, such as war (Ps 3), sickness (Ps 6), and oppression of the poor (Ps 10). Whatever the problem or complaint, the petitioner speaks in the first-person, as an "I" in a covenantal relationship with a "You," namely God's very self. This relationship is intimate and deep, so much so that the petitioner can make heavy demands on God and even command God to respond. Several psalms make it clear that the petitioner is very angry at God's apparent unconcern or deafness to their pleas (Ps 13).

The laments assert that something is not right in the individual's life or in the community. They maintain that the intolerable situation can and must change. They also contend that God must bring about the transformation. The laments bring to the fore a personal grievance, an unjust system, a wrong that needs to be rectified, and mobilize God to action. They redistribute power between the parties of the covenant by demanding God keep God's part of the covenant. The one who prays is not silenced, but taken seriously, empowered to bring his or her crises and troubles to God. These painful crises also offer a context for praising God in the laments, because the petitioner knows in faith that God has helped in the past and will provide in the future.

The convention of the petitioner speaking in the first-person allows both genders to come before God in a lament. In addition, the troubles, tribulations, and enemies in the Psalms are vague enough to apply to a range of gender-specific contexts. We saw this in our interpretation of Psalm 55 as a psalm of a battered woman pleading for God's help. The pain from her abuse, her desire to escape, the naming of her marital perpetrator, her courage to call upon God—all these aspects of her experience can be read into this psalm. I hope this exercise opens our hearts and imaginations to using the book of Psalms in our own prayer lives.

IMPLICATIONS FOR THE PULPIT TODAY

It should be clear that I strongly urge ministers to preach from the book of Psalms. Eucharists in my tradition follow the lectionary readings that have an Old Testament reading first, followed by a psalm response to it, then a secondary reading, usually from the Epistles, and finally the Gospel. In my experience at Eucharist, sermons from the pulpit rarely preach on the Old Testament reading, much less the psalm response. Rather, sermons usually go straight to the Gospel reading. There is a richness of stories from the Old Testament that congregations are missing. Furthermore, never preaching from the collection of prayers from the book of Psalms impoverishes their spiritual life.

As I have tried to show, the first-person "I" speaker allows both men and women to find their prayer lives enriched by the psalms. Psalms cover a wide range of passionate emotions that both genders experience. Their lack of details allows the psalms to be applied in any number of troubles and sufferings that humans undergo, so that God can hear them. Additionally, the Psalms can be applied to adversities that are specific to women in particular. Preaching Psalm 55, as we did from the standpoint of a domestic-violence victim, will support and help those invisible victims in the pews to find a way to pray to God themselves.

Ultimately, the Psalms exhibit a range of emotions that many members of our congregations are already feeling: helplessness, abandonment, anxiety, sorrow, joy, thanksgiving, praise, and many others. Preaching from the Psalms will encourage our congregations to look to the Psalms for their own devotional prayer life.

IMPLICATIONS FOR TODAY'S PULPIT

1. Have you preached from the book of Psalms? Why or why not?

2. Are the Psalms a part of your personal prayer life? Part of your congregation's prayer life?

3. Have you given Bible studies on the book of Psalms?

4. What are the two main literary types of psalms?

5. When you pray, do they fit these literary types? Why or why not?

6. How did you respond to the reading of Psalm 55 as a prayer from a victim of domestic violence?

7. Take a psalm. Read it over and over again. Is it a song of praise or a lament? Does the psalm resonate with any part of your life experience?

BIBLIOGRAPHY

Bail, Ulrike. "'O God, Hear My Prayer': Psalm 55 and Violence against Women." In *Wisdom and the Psalms*, edited by Athalya Brenner and Carole R. Fontaine, 242–63. A Feminist Companion to the Bible, 2nd ser. Sheffield: Sheffield Academic, 1998.

Boney M. "Rivers of Babylon." *YouTube.* Music video, 3:39. https://youtu.be/2FgDles4xq8/.

Brueggemann, Walter. "The Costly Loss of Lament." *Journal for the Study of the Old Testament* 36 (1986) 57–71.

Kaufman, Ivan T. "Undercut by Joy: The Sunday Lectionaries and the Psalms of Lament." In *The Psalms and Other Studies on the Old Testament*, edited by Jack C. Knight and Lawrence A. Sinclair, 66–78. Nashotah, WI: Nashotah House Seminary, 1990.

The Melodians. "Rivers of Babylon." Official audio. *YouTube.* Music video, 3:29. https://youtu.be/BXf1j8Hz2bU/.

Ronstadt, Linda. "Rivers of Babylon." *YouTube.* Music video, 0:53. https://youtu.be/bGusDqcCfE8/.

3

Valorous and Wise
Women Who Build Up the House of God

EUNNY P. LEE

I WILL ALWAYS REMEMBER Prof. Alan Neely's World Christianity course at Princeton Theological Seminary because of the student information form that he circulated at the beginning of the term. This first-day ritual is usually perfunctory and unremarkable. But in addition to the typical questions one expects, Prof. Neely's form also featured what I thought was a rather personal question, "What are the biggest challenges you are currently facing in your household?" After gathering up our responses, he turned to the class and asked, "How many of you answered, poverty, famine, displacement from home, or prostitution and human trafficking . . . ?" He let this even more personal follow-up question linger in the room before suggesting that if we had *not* included any of those things, we were operating with a notion of home that was far too narrow. That unexpected shift challenged the class to see the church as a household that spans the globe; the suffering in other corners of the world was also our suffering (1 Cor 12:26).

Another memorable moment in that course was Dr. Samuel Moffett's and his wife Eileen's visit to the class. They had come to speak about the history of Christianity in Asia and their own experience as missionaries in South Korea. In the midst of her comments, Mrs. Moffett joyfully announced that the Presbyterian Church of Korea had just ordained their first woman as minister of Word and sacrament. It was 1996 and my second year in the MDiv program. I had grown up in the Korean American Presbyterian church, with its traditional views on gender roles, and at the time, I still had misgivings about women's leadership in the church, particularly when it came to ordination. But I had enormous respect for Eileen Moffett, and the joy with which she celebrated this long-awaited milestone led me to reexamine the issue—and the biblical teaching on the issue—with a new curiosity.

So began my journey toward embracing women's ministries in all forms, and more fundamentally, gender equality in all spheres of life. The two experiences above transformed the way I think about the household of God.

Asian American and Pacific Islander (AAPI) and Latino/a churches in the United States have historically embraced theological perspectives that honor the dignity of ethnic differences, striving to create communities— including faith communities—that recognize and value all our voices and our experiences. However, when it comes to the voices of women in our pulpits, many of our churches lag behind. Often this hesitation is rooted in traditional views about gender roles that purportedly are founded in Scripture. Yet Scripture itself invites each generation to reexamine our traditions critically, in light of what the Bible teaches. Indeed, we must read both our sacred texts and our traditions critically, with openness to what the Spirit may be saying anew to our churches. For AAPI and Latino/a churches, this kind of engagement propels us to expand our vision of a diverse and inclusive church to more fully embrace the gifts that women bring to our pulpits.

In this chapter, I invite you to explore with me a cluster of texts from the books of Ruth and Proverbs that portray women *against* the grain of traditional gender stereotypes. These two Old Testament books feature "valorous women" (Hebrew *'eshet hayil*: Ruth 3:11; Prov 31:10; cf. Prov 12:4; 31:29) and their vital roles in building up households, broadly conceived. Both Ruth and the woman of Proverbs 31 are lifted up as paradigms of covenant faithfulness (*hesed*) for the community. Moreover, they are critical for the survival—and flourishing—of their houses, and are *publicly* celebrated for it.

Let me begin by briefly laying out some of the principles of biblical interpretation that have transformed my own understanding of Scripture and how it might speak to us in our ongoing work toward an equal pulpit.

41

1. Reading the Bible is a cross-cultural enterprise. Biblical texts were written long ago, in faraway places, and in languages that are utterly foreign to most of us. As preachers and teachers in the church, we need to respect the "otherness" of the text and do our best to make sense of the language of the Bible in its own cultural and literary contexts. Rather than accepting traditional interpretations that have been handed down to us, we must reexamine them critically within the biblical context. To cite a classic example, when we read in Genesis 2:20 that the woman was created as a "helper corresponding to" the man, it is important to consider what "helper" signifies in the *biblical* world. Many of my students have an aha moment when they learn that in the Old Testament, "helper" most frequently refers to God. Hence, Eve's role as Adam's helper does not indicate her subordinate status, but her unique ability to render help that is vital for his existence.

2. If we respect the "otherness" of these ancient texts, we must also acknowledge their androcentric bias. The book of Proverbs, for example, originally addressed a male audience, as evident in the vocative "my son" or "sons" that recurs throughout the instructions (1:8, 10, 15; 2:1; 3:1, 11, 21; 4:1, 10; 5:1, 7, 20; 6:3, 20; 7:1, 24; 8:31; 23:15, 19, 26; 24:13, 21; 27:11; cf. 31:2). Contemporary translations render these terms as "child/children" to open up the audience for the book. But the masculine forms remind us that Proverbs was originally intended as instruction for young men on the cusp of adulthood. The book's symbolic world thus imagines women in binary categories (either wholly good or wholly bad), according to how they may or may not benefit the man. At the same time, however, Proverbs brings the concept of wisdom to life by portraying it as a Woman, calling readers to ponder the relationship between wisdom and the feminine.

3. Given the Bible's androcentric bias, we must listen closely if we want to discern what it has to say to, for, and about women. And we must do so even when it becomes uncomfortable and painful. When we encounter troubling texts of daughters being sacrificed (Judg 11) or concubines being raped and dismembered (Judg 19–21), we *bear witness* to those who suffer in the narrative. We must not whitewash or ignore these "texts of terror," but confront them honestly and be outraged by the injustice and the violence.[1] As we attend closely to these

---

1. Trible, *Texts of Terror.*

biblical stories, we cultivate our capacity to attend to similar stories of violence in our world.

4. In other words, not everything in the Bible is meant to be *prescriptive* for us today. Often the Bible is to be read *descriptively*. That is, biblical narratives give us a true depiction of the human condition and the complex challenges of living in a broken world with broken people. Think of the various Old Testament narratives where women use trickery and sexuality to force a man's hand to do right by them (see Gen 19:30–38; 29:21–30; 38:6–26; Ruth 3). Do we now encourage women to model their lives around these stories?[2] Surely not. At the same time, it is important to note that the biblical narratives do not condemn such tactics. Rather, they memorialize the desperate struggles of women who have few or no other options, who risk everything just to survive. As we enter into these stories and allow them to shape our moral response, they move us to care more deeply about the unjust socioeconomic structures that place women in a similar plight today.

5. Despite its male-centered orientation, the Old Testament also *speaks a liberating word for women*. The *foundational* testimony of Scripture affirms the equal partnership of men and women, who together reflect the image of God (Gen 1:27). If we take seriously the hermeneutical principle that scripture interprets scripture, then we need to evaluate every text in light of that theological claim. But because the concerns of women are often buried in between or beneath the lines of Scripture, we must train our ears to listen more closely for this "whispered word."[3]

To that end, I now turn to the books of Ruth and Proverbs. Each section of this study will begin with a series of questions designed to help the reader listen more closely to the "whispered word" for women. A commentary on a selection of texts will then explore the imagery of women and their agency as builders of their houses and, by extension, the house of God.

2. Katherine Doob Sakenfeld recounts the story of a young girl in the Philippines who decides to work as a dancer in a foreign country to earn money for her family. She justifies her decision by citing the example of Ruth, who put herself in a compromising position to secure her marriage to Boaz. She would do the same in the hopes that God would lead her to a rich benefactor. See Sakenfeld, *Just Wives?*, 35.

3. See Lapsley, *Whispering the Word*.

RUTH: REIMAGINING THE HOUSEHOLD OF GOD

Many are familiar with the book of Ruth, which tells the story of a Bethle-hem household facing extinction through a series of catastrophes: famine, displacement, childlessness, and the death of its men (1:1–5). With the loss of their husbands, Naomi and her Moabite daughter-in-law become vul-nerable widows. But this loss also enables them to emerge as the primary actors in the story as they find ways to survive and preserve their "house." And, it turns out, their survival is critical not only for them but for the larger biblical story, because nothing less than the house of *David*—so cen-tral to the Bible as a whole—is at stake (4:17, 18–22). In the end, the family is preserved by the women's resourcefulness and Ruth's marriage to Boaz, Naomi's kinsman-redeemer.

The study below will focus on the climactic moment of the story, when the community of Bethlehem celebrates the union of Ruth and Boaz (4:11–12).

Questions for Close Reading: Ruth 4

Read the book of Ruth in its entirety. Then read chapter 4 again, with the following questions in mind:

1. How does the resolution of the story come about? Who are the agents in the transaction that happens at the city gate? Who is present and who is absent?

2. The word "house" occurs five times in the blessing, signaling its im-portance. What observations can you make about how this thematic word functions in the text?

3. In the climactic blessing of the community (4:11–12), the story of Ruth is placed in the context of Israel's larger story. Indeed, some in-terpreters have suggested that the blessing itself is a retelling of that metanarrative in brief. How does this blessing summarize that larger story? Who are the main actors in this summary? What does that sug-gest about God's providential activity on behalf of Israel (and more broadly, the people of God)?

4. How is this retelling in Ruth 4:11–12 different from the story you know from the ancestral narratives in Genesis? How is it similar?

What do the differences between Ruth 4:11–12 and Genesis suggest about the role of women in building "houses" in ancient Israel?

The community blessing first focuses on Ruth as she is about to enter Boaz's household. Her incorporation into this family is remarkable, given her Moabite "baggage," as biblical narratives display an animosity toward Moab in general and an unease about Moabite women in particular (Gen 19:30–38; Num 22; 25:1–5; Judg 3; Jer 48; Ezra 9–10; Neh 13). Because of this ancient hostility, Deut 23:3–6 forbids Moabites from entering Israel's religious assembly, and this prohibition later becomes the rationale for excommunicating foreign wives in the books of Ezra and Nehemiah.[4] The book of Ruth, however, paints a very different picture. Moab provides for a hungry Israelite family (contra Deut 23:4). Moabite women are elevated as paragons of covenant faithfulness (*hesed*, 1:8). And the marriage of a destitute Moabite widow to a prominent man of Bethlehem is celebrated as a good match. When Boaz recognizes Ruth to be "a woman of worth" (*'eshet hayil*, 3:11), the narrative signals that she is indeed a fitting counterpart for this "man of great worth" (*'ish gibbor hayil*, 2:2).

The Hebrew word *hayil* has several nuances (as we will see in Proverbs 31). When it is used to describe Boaz in 2:2, it denotes his socioeconomic stature as a wealthy man of high standing. Meanwhile, Ruth is a destitute widow. Her "worth" is demonstrated in the industry and energy with which she faithfully provides for herself and for Naomi (chapter 2).

The blessing hints at the consequential nature of the union. Pointing back to Israel's founding mothers and forward to the founding of David's dynasty, the marriage signals an important moment not only for the book of Ruth but also for the community's larger story.[5] The fate of this household is bound up with Israel's destiny. The connections are reinforced by the central motif of "house" or *bayit*. The Hebrew word *bayit* may refer to a physical residence (Boaz's house; Bethlehem, literally "house of bread"), but also to the family that occupies it (Boaz's progeny). *Bayit* takes on a broader meaning when it refers to the descendants of a particular tribe or

---

4. The book of Ruth also registers this anxiety about Moab, but more subtly, through a recurring emphasis on the Moabite Ruth's ethnicity (1:22; 2:2, 6, 21; 4:5, 10) and an insistent interrogation of Ruth's identity (2:5; 3:9, 16; cf. 1:19). But those who question Ruth are forced to reevaluate their constructions of identity and difference.

5. One scholar argues that continuity of people and land is the Hebrew Bible's overarching theme, which reaches a critical moment here in Ruth. Berlin, "Ruth and the Continuity of Israel," 255–60.

clan ("house of Perez"), or even the Israelite people as a whole ("house of Israel"). When the house in question belongs to a king, it can signify a palace
or a dynasty, a usage that is clearly in view here via the Davidic genealogy
that concludes the book (4:17–22).

Although the community blessing does not mention Ruth the Moabite
by name, they liken her to Israel's matriarchs and acknowledge her critical
role in the ongoing flourishing of Israel's house.[6] The story's remarkable
vision of kinship reaching across ethnic boundaries calls us to imagine an
expansive house that welcomes all. This is a vision that AAPI and Latinx
faith communities gladly embrace. Biblical narratives like Ruth pave the
way for the house that Jesus describes in Luke 13, which subverts our pre-
conceptions of who's in and who's out, so that "people will come from east
and west, from north and south, and will eat in the kingdom of God" (vv.
25, 29).

The biblical witness concerning "open houses" pushes us even further. What is especially striking about this blessing is its public acclaim of
women as the primary *builders* of the house of Israel. Moreover, the blessing concludes with the declaration that Boaz's thriving household will be
actualized through "the seed which YHWH will grant you from this young
woman." The structure of this blessing thus echoes the larger theological
framework of the book, which begins and ends with a narrative report-
ing of God's providential activity. The story begins in earnest when God
overturns the problem of the barren land and provides bread for the people
of Bethlehem (1:6); it comes to a close when God overturns the problem
of a barren couple and provides a child (4:13). God's "giving" thus frames
the narrative. In the remainder of the book, God remains largely "in the
shadows," yielding the stage to courageous women who take the initiative
to secure their future, and to a God-centered man who recognizes their
valor (2:11; 3:11).

That same structure is evident in the community blessing:

> May YHWH grant that the woman coming into your house
> be like Rachel and Leah, who together built the house of Israel.

6. Ruth contains a number of subtle allusions to the ancestral narratives: a famine-
driven migration into a foreign land that threatens the safety of Israel's matriarchs ("there
was a famine in the land" only at Gen 12:10; 26:1; and Ruth 1:1); Naomi's use of the
divine epithet "Shaddai" in 1:20–21 (traditionally rendered as "Almighty"), which is associated with the promise of fecundity in Gen 28:3; 35:11; 49:25; the intertextual echoes
of Tamar's story (Gen 38) in Ruth 3. The references, however, become explicit in 4:11–12,
which I will discuss more fully below.

Thus may you flourish in Ephrathah!
Thus may you proclaim a name in Bethlehem!
May your house be like the house of Perez whom Tamar bore to Judah
from the seed which YHWH will grant you from this young woman.

(4:11–12, author's translation)

A twofold reference to YHWH's "giving" surrounds and grounds the blessing by asking YHWH to grant that Ruth build like Rachel and Leah, and
then bear children like Tamar. Here, the blessing recognizes that God's gift
is actualized through female agency. YHWH's "giving" is parallel to wom-
en's "building" and "bearing," indicating a shared agency at work in the
founding of this house. Indeed, the book's theological orientation valorizes
the agency of those who are commonly excluded from the main action.

Women are of course needed to produce children. But Israel's matriarchs are credited with *building* the house of Israel. The language is remarkable, given that the subject of the verb is typically male. Important houses
are built by men of royal or priestly background (2 Sam 5:9; 1 Kgs 5–9,
passim; Neh 3:1). Even ordinary homes have male builders (e.g., Deut 25:9).
Ultimately, however, building houses is God's prerogative. As the psalmist
declares, "Unless the LORD builds the house, those who build it labor in
vain" (Ps 127:1). The accent on divine prerogative is even more prominent
in 2 Sam 7, where YHWH disallows David's lofty plans to build a house
for God (v. 5), and pledges instead to establish a house for David (vv. 11,
16, 27). This text too plays on the multiple meanings of "house" (Hebrew:
bayit) David's offspring will eventually build a temple (*bayit*) for YHWH,
but even that will signify YHWH's faithfulness in establishing David's royal
line (*bayit*).[7] Indeed, 2 Sam 7 is a comprehensive recital of God's beneficent
activity on behalf of David, in which God claims all the action (twenty-
three verbs) and puts the king in his proper place.

In Ruth 4:11–12, divine action embraces and promotes women who
build. Rachel, Leah, and Tamar all ensure their family's continuity, sometimes despite their husbands. The Genesis narratives, however, tend to
highlight the painful and unflattering dimensions of their stories. In the
case of Rachel and Leah, their bitter rivalry drives the narrative.[8] Feminist

7. There are additional intertextual echoes between this text and Ruth. The house that
YHWH establishes for David is characterized by secure rootedness, signified by the notion of "rest" (cf. Ruth 1:9; 3:1). References to the "great name" (2 Sam 7:9; Ruth 4:11, 14)
and to Ephrathah (1 Sam 17:12; Ruth 4:11; cf. 1:2) also reinforce the Davidic connection.

8. Tamar resorts to trickery and prostitution (Gen 38). But the scandalous elements
of these stories may function as a critique of the patriarchal culture that places women

interpreters point instead to a hidden cooperation beneath the surface of the text (see Gen 30:14–15).[9] The claim in Ruth 4:11 that the two sisters *together* built the house of Israel pays tribute to their collaboration. Indeed, the portrayal of the bonding between Ruth and Naomi throughout the book offers an "idyllic revision" of the Genesis rivalry.[10]

By attending to the female *togetherness* noted in Ruth 4:11, feminist critics have thus recovered a suppressed element in the biblical narrative— the female solidarity that enables Israel's growth. But just as important is the extraordinary claim that these women "*built* the house of Israel." In Genesis, Israel's foremothers appear as subjects of the verb *banah* when, unable to bear offspring of their own, they attempt "to be built up" through surrogates (Sarah in Gen 16:2; Rachel in Gen 30:3).[11] The passive verb highlights the helplessness of these reproductively challenged women. But in Ruth 4:11, the matriarchs are transformed from passive objects to active subjects who are able to exercise creative power of their own. The text recasts their struggle positively. Their initiative and their agency receive appropriate recognition in this alternative account of Israel's origins. Ruth's revisionism thus highlights not just collaboration among women, but also between women and God. The matriarchs are acknowledged as the master builders of the house of Israel, empowered by God the chief architect. Women work in concert with one another, and in concert with God, to build up Israel.

The heart of the blessing focuses on the flourishing of Boaz's household into the future (cf. 4:14, 4:17–22). But the man's interests cannot be divorced from the woman's. Indeed, the dominant note sounded by the blessing is a celebration of God's work in and through women. This emphasis on women's agency is altogether in keeping with a book that acknowledges the importance of the "mother's house" (1:8). The maternal attribution is quite unusual (it occurs elsewhere only in Gen 24:28; Song 3:4; 8:2). Much more common is the notion of the "father's house." But the notion of a "mother's house" surfaces in texts that feature female voices and their agency. These occurrences signal the possibility that Israelite women played "a role equal to if not greater than their husbands" in the domestic

---

in such desperate straits.

9. Klagsbrun, "Ruth and Naomi, Rachel and Leah," 264.

10. Pardes, *Countertraditions in the Bible*, 98–117.

11. The expression "that I may have children through her" (NRSV) literally reads in Hebrew, "that I may be built up through her."

setting of the household and even beyond.[12] The references to "mother's house" and women "builders" in Ruth thus prompt readers to rehabilitate the agency of women, indelibly inscribed even within the male-centered discourse of ancient Israel.

Ruth's theology of providence thus features a God who gives and shares agency. God acts behind the scenes, enabling women to emerge as the preeminent builders of the house of Israel. In Ruth 4:11–12, the house that Rachel and Leah built together opens to welcome a foreigner within its fold and gives her a share in the work of building up Israel. *The openness of this house reflects God's own willingness to yield power and space to his human partners.* Indeed, it is by YHWH's "grant" (Hebrew: *natan*, 4:11) that Ruth enters this house and joins the ranks of Israel's matriarchs.

THE VALOROUS WOMAN OF PROVERBS 31 AND HER HOUSE

It is easy, nevertheless, to downplay the significance of women builders in Ruth if we tie their building activity narrowly to their reproductive abilities. Bearing children is an important aspect of building households, but just as important is the ongoing work of nurturing and raising the young to maturity, tending to the family's needs, and directing the moral formation of children. In other words, women build households through a wide range of activities that involve wisdom and skill.

The full array of these activities is depicted in the book of Proverbs, where a feminine brand of wisdom is the key ingredient for building houses. Indeed, Proverbs offers an invaluable resource for contemporary theology and questions about women's role in the church because of the prominence of women in the book. Wisdom itself is personified as a commanding female figure (Prov 1:20–33; 4:5–9; 7:4–5; 8:1–36; 9:1–6) who "builds her house" and calls everyone with ears to hear to enter and live (9:1–6; cf. 24:3–4). The book also features a supporting cast of wise women who are guideposts along the way to wisdom.[13] Prov 14:1 thus declares, "The manifold wisdom of women builds her house." The NRSV rendering, "The wise woman builds her house," obscures the plural forms present in

---

12. Meyers, "Returning Home."

13. Various "types" of women—wise women as well as foolish and "strange" women—play an important role in the symbolic world of Proverbs.

the Hebrew text.[14] The saying deliberately builds on the language regarding Wisdom's house in 9:1 and establishes an integral connection between the heavenly figure who was present with God at the creation of the world (8:22–31) and real women who display the same wisdom in their own creative activities. This association between wisdom and the feminine suggests that women—who they are and what they do—are a matter of profound theological significance for the life of God's people.

Finally, when the book of Proverbs draws to a close, the journey toward wisdom ends at the "house" of a remarkable woman who is the very embodiment of wisdom (31:15, 21, 27). And yet, the poem in Prov 31:10–31 has posed challenges for women readers. I have heard women describing this figure as a "mental nemesis," a role model who has become an impossible measuring stick. Moreover, her strengths are too often tied to her role as wife and mother. Single and childless women may feel alienated. I know of a woman who stopped going to church on Mother's Day because her pastor would invariably preach from this text, and she could not bear to be reminded of the "ideal" that was beyond her reach. Others have found this woman unappealing because of the way she orients her life around her husband's interests. She thus enables the social structures that continue to underprivilege women. How do we rehabilitate this figure so that she may speak to and for women today?

Questions for Close Reading: Proverbs 31:10–31

1. Compare the NRSV and NIV translations of 31:10. How is this woman named? Given the multiple dimensions of the Hebrew word *hayil* noted above, it is possible to render the expression *'eshet hayil* as "a valorous woman." How does that rendering impact your reading of the poem? Based on the description of the woman's activities in the poem, which option do you think is the most apt for this woman?

2. The poem in 31:10–31 is an alphabetic acrostic (the first line begins with the first letter of the Hebrew alphabet, the second line the second letter, and so on). What do you think this literary form says about how we are to read the poem?

14. The plural of "wisdom" (*hokmot*) may be taken as a plural of majesty or complexity (cf. Prov 1:20; 9:1, and so forth for personified Wisdom).

3. What kinds of activity are attributed to this woman? How would you describe the scope of her activity and her sphere of influence? Pay special attention to the imagery of the woman's hand/palm, the symbol of her agency.

4. Read Proverbs 31:1–9. What verbal echoes do you detect between that text and the poem in 31:10–31? How does this literary context inform the way you read the latter?

5. Read Proverbs 1:20–33; 3:13–20; 8:1–36; 9: 1–6. What resonances do you detect between the portrait of personified Wisdom in those texts and the woman of Proverbs 31? How do these connections inform your understanding of the "valorous woman"?

The poem in 31:10–31 sings the praises of a heroic woman in the form of an alphabetic acrostic that catalogues her many achievements from *A* to *Z*, and holds her up as the "perfect" embodiment of wisdom and of the fear of the Lord. Who is this woman? Most English translations render the Hebrew expression *'eshet hayil* as "a virtuous wife" (KJV), "a capable wife" (NRSV), "a wife of noble character" (NIV), or the like. But these appellations flatten the meaning of the Hebrew text. The noun *hayil* is a multivalent word, which may refer to various forms of strength, including military might, socioeconomic influence, intellectual power, and strong moral character. When the term is applied to men, it is often rendered as "mighty" or "valiant." But those attributives are just as fitting for the woman of Proverbs 31, who marshals her energy, courage, and resourcefulness to secure the well-being of her household.

That sense of strength is created by the poem's use of words typically associated with warriors and victors in battle. Verse 11 declares that because of her, her husband "lacks no *booty*," a term that almost always denotes the spoils of war. Similarly, she provides food—literally, "prey"—for her household (v. 15). This surprising term evokes the imagery of a hunter or a lioness who displays physical prowess in tracking down her quarry. The overtones suggest that this woman is a woman of adventure and daring, who seeks out ways to protect and provide for her household, even in the face of significant obstacles. She "girds herself with strength, and makes her arms strong" for the challenge (v. 17). Thus, notes one interpreter, "If ancient Israel admired the man of war (even Yahweh in Exod 15:1–3) who defended God's people from their enemies, and if Israelite males, like men throughout history, were sinfully prone to demean women as 'the weaker sex,' the praise of woman here is designed to alter errant male perceptions of women."[15]

Indeed, the valorous woman is strong in every sense of the word. She pursues an astounding array of activities: negotiating with merchants, handpicking quality goods, surveying and acquiring land, planting vineyards, fitting and supplying "*her* house" with all that it needs (vv. 13–16). It is important to remember that in ancient Israelite society (as in many agrarian societies today), the household was the primary economic unit. There was no separation of home and work, and women held major economic responsibilities.[16] Proverbs 31 thus depicts the woman as an efficient manager and provider. And this woman takes pleasure in her work and savors her accomplishments (vv. 13, 18, 25). This portrayal is an important corrective to the common stereotype that women in ancient Israel were sequestered, subservient, and severely restricted in their personal independence. That is not to say that they enjoyed socioeconomic equality with men; ancient Israelite society was largely patriarchal.[17] But neither were they "just wives and mothers." Their activities went far beyond childbearing and domestic chores. In Proverbs 31, the woman's base of operations is the home, but she moves nimbly beyond it into the world. Indeed, her scope of action spans all of creation, as she traverses land (v. 16) and sea (v. 14) to gather resources for her house.[18] She takes active part in the mandate to fill the earth with her creativity and to "master" it (Gen 1:28–29).

All this she does not only for her family's benefit, but for the larger public good (vv. 17, 20, 24, 31). With one hand she weaves garments to clothe her household (vv. 13, 19, 21–22); with the other she cares for the poor and the needy (v. 20), weaving together the bonds of society. Moreover, the woman exercises moral and religious authority: "She opens her mouth with wisdom, and the teaching (*torah*) of covenant faithfulness is on her tongue" (v. 26). In other words, she takes on the role traditionally associated with the priesthood. This poem is typically dated to the period after the Babylonian exile, a period in Israel's history when its national and religious institutions had suffered collapse. In their place, the home and

15. Van Leeuwen, "Building God's House," 264.

16. See Meyers, *Rediscovering Eve*. For an extended analysis of woman of Proverbs 31, see Yoder, *Wisdom as a Woman of Substance*. She argues that the portrait of the "woman of substance" was modeled on the lives of actual Israelite women of the Persian period.

17. See Kay Arthur's discussion of patriarchy in Chapter 1.

18. Van Leeuwen, "Building God's House," 261.

the local community became the central locus for religious formation. So, perhaps it is not surprising that the woman would take the lead in the education of her children. But v. 26 is open-ended, suggesting that the scope of her instruction need not be limited to her household.[19]

It is also significant that this poem directly follows the instructions of a royal mother to her son Lemuel (31:1–9), with which it shares a number of striking verbal resonances. Like the queen mother who directs her son to "open your mouth" for the sake of "the poor and needy" (vv. 1, 8–9), the valorous woman "opens her mouth," not only to teach but also model the ways of justice and covenant faithfulness (vv. 20, 26). The echoes suggest that her influence reaches beyond the narrow circle of home. Hence, the poem declares that she is adorned with "power and dignity" (v. 25), the attire of royalty (Pss 21:5; cf. 8:5) and even of God (Pss 29:1; 93:1; 104:1; Job 40:10). Finally, the poem concludes with an emphatic call to give the woman the public recognition and acclaim she deserves (v. 31).[20]

Indeed, that urgent appeal is the final word of the book of Proverbs. The poem about the valorous woman thus serves as the book's conclusion. And it shares numerous echoes with the extended introduction to the book in Proverbs 1–9, where Woman Wisdom is a dominant figure. Both female figures

are more precious than rubies (31:10; 3:15; 8:11)

produce "profit and wealth" (31:11, 18; 3:14; 8:18, 21)

produce "fruit" (31:16, 31; 8:19)

oversee a thriving household (31:15, 21, 27; 8:34; 9:1; cf. 14:1)

supply their houses with food (31:14; 9:5)

speak wisdom and faithful teaching (31:26; 8:6–9)

have honor (31:25, 28–31; 3:16; 8:18; cf. 11:16)

possess strength (3:17, 25; 8:14)

19. Note that the woven goods she produces for her house are the same as the precious items used for the building of God's "house" in Exodus (28:5; 35:25). The "wisdom" of women builds up her own home and her community; it also builds up the house of God.

20. The "gate" represents the legal assembly of the town, where its male citizens determine important judicial and economic cases (see also 31:23; cf. Ruth 4:1–12). It is a locus of male power and privilege. Here, the poem calls for a public and authoritative recognition of the woman's power (cf. 3:11, where the Hebrew term is translated as "assembly").

So, who is the woman of Proverbs 31? Is she a real woman, or is she the personification of wisdom? The lines between the two are blurred. She embodies all of the values (from *A* to *Z*) that have been commended by the sages in the book. In v. 30, her crowning virtue is the fear of the Lord, just as wisdom itself begins *and* culminates in the fear of the Lord (1:7; 9:10; 2:5). Yet there is a concrete dimension to this figure, that honors the activities of real women as constitutive of wisdom. Taken together, the valorous woman and Woman Wisdom positively reinforce each other. The wise woman in Proverbs 31 is accorded profound value by her intimate association with Wisdom, and Wisdom is humanized and given concrete, practical expression in the daily life of the woman.

The houses that real women build (cf. Prov 14:1) reflect the house that Wisdom builds (Prov 9:1), a seven-pillared house that offers life in all its fullness.[21] Scholars have debated the significance of the seven pillars. Are they intended to depict the expansiveness of this house, like the house of a prosperous noble woman? Do they denote the columns of a temple? Or do they signify the foundations of the cosmos itself (Ps 75:3; cf. 1 Sam 2:8; Job 9:6; 26:11)? The imagery is deliberately ambiguous, making it amenable to all of these interpretations.

Elsewhere in the Old Testament, the imagery of building often surfaces in texts about creation.[22] These texts make clear that building houses—of various kinds—implies skillful craftsmanship. In Proverbs 3:19–20, God constructs the world as a master architect would build a house or a city, laying the foundation, establishing a firm structure, and arranging the great cosmic spaces to support life. And he does so with "wisdom," "intelligence," and "knowledge" (cf. Job 12:13–14; Pss 104:24; 136:5; Isa 40:14; Jer 10:12; 51:15). Remarkably, these same three words, in this same precise order, occur in the description of the building of God's home on earth. Indeed, both the tabernacle and Solomon's temple are built with "wisdom, intelligence, and knowledge" in every kind of work (Exod 31:1–3; 35:30–31; 36:1; 1 Kgs 7:14;). These intertextual echoes suggest that the construction of the tabernacle and the Solomonic temple were to be modeled after God's own

21. On the significance of Wisdom personified as a woman, see Camp, *Wisdom and the Feminine in the Book of Proverbs*.

22. The close association between building and wisdom may explain the Talmudic interpretation of Gen 2:22, where God is said to "build" Eve as a fitting counterpart for Adam. The Talmud invokes the resonances between the language of divine "building" (Heb. *banah*) and "understanding" (Heb. *binah*) to conclude that God granted women a greater wisdom than men (b. Niddah 45b).

"building" of creation (Exod 31:12–17; 35:1–3; 1 Kgs 6:38).[23] Moreover, in the case of the tabernacle, all who are skilled (literally "wise of heart") in their craft, including women skilled in weaving, are called to apply their expertise and participate in the creative work of building (Exod 35:10, 25, 35). The proficient construction of any house presupposes harmony with God's own creative work. It is meant to reflect the wisdom with which God built the cosmos.

God created this world in wisdom. All of our building efforts—whether temple building or home building—are to be modeled after God's building activity, which valorizes the creative agency of wise women. In Proverbs, Woman Wisdom raises her prophetic voice to issue an urgent call to learn from her (1:20–33; cf. 9:3). She calls loudly because so many are hard of hearing. To respond to the call to honor the strengths of women (31:31) is to respond to none other than Wisdom itself and the will of God.

I hope that these close reading exercises have demonstrated that the Bible offers us a compelling theological warrant for affirming an "equal pulpit." The book of Ruth depicts women as partners with God in building up the house of Israel and ensuring the flourishing of God's people. The book of Proverbs echoes that claim and broadens our understanding of this house to include not only the domestic sphere but also public spheres traditionally associated with male leadership. Recognizing the full range of gifts that women bring to our churches and to our pulpits will only make our "houses" stronger and wiser. Let those with ears—in AAPI and Latino churches—hear what our Scriptures may teach us about the wisdom and valor of women and their place in our churches.

Questions for Group Discussion:

1. How did the close reading of Ruth 4 and Proverbs 31 impact your understanding of the Bible's teachings regarding women's role in the church? What new insight did you gain that may have challenged or nuanced your prior understanding? What questions remain for you?

2. How might you teach and preach the stories of biblical women to encourage others in your church to embrace the voices of women in the pulpit?

---

23. See Van Leeuwen, "Building God's House."

BIBLIOGRAPHY

Berlin, Adele. "Ruth and the Continuity of Israel." In *Reading Ruth: Contemporary Women Reclaim a Sacred Story,* edited by Judith A. Kates and Gail Twersky Reimer, 255–60. New York: Ballantine, 1994.

Camp, Claudia V. *Wisdom and the Feminine in the Book of Proverbs.* Bible and Literature 11. Sheffield: Almond, 1985.

Klagsbrun, Francine. "Ruth and Naomi, Rachel and Leah: Sisters under the Skin." In *Reading Ruth: Contemporary Women Reclaim a Sacred Story,* edited by Judith A. Kates and Gail Twersky Reimer, 262–71. New York: Ballantine, 1994.

Lapsley, Jacqueline E. *Whispering the Word: Hearing Women's Stories in the Old Testament.* Louisville: Westminster John Knox, 2005.

Meyers, Carol. "Returning Home: Ruth 1:8 and the Gendering of the Book of Ruth." In *Feminist Companion to Ruth,* edited by Athalya Brenner, 85–115. Feminist Companion to the Bible 3. Sheffield: Sheffield Academic, 1993.

———. *Rediscovering Eve: Ancient Israelite Women in Context.* Oxford: Oxford University Press, 2013.

Pardes, Ilana. *Countertraditions in the Bible: A Feminist Approach.* Cambridge: Harvard University Press, 1992.

Trible, Phyllis. *Texts of Terror: Literary-Feminist Readings of Biblical Narratives.* Overtures to Biblical Theology. Philadelphia: Fortress, 1984.

Van Leeuwen, Raymond C. "Building God's House: An Exploration in Wisdom." In *The Way of Wisdom: Essays in Honor of Bruce K. Waltke,* edited by J. I. Packer and Sven K. Soderlund, 204–11. Grand Rapids: Zondervan, 2000.

———. "Proverbs." In *The New Interpreter's Bible.* Vol. 5, *Proverbs–Sirach,* edited by Leander E. Keck, 17–264. 13 vols. Nashville: Abingdon, 1997.

Yoder, Christine Roy. *Wisdom as a Woman of Substance: A Socioeconomic Reading of Proverbs 1–9 and 31:10–31.* Beihefte zur Zeitschrift für die alttestamentliche Wissenschaft 304. Berlin: de Gruyter, 2001.

4

Listening for Your Voice; Let Me Hear It

The Prophetic Feminine Voice in Songs 8

SOPHIA MAGALLANES-TSANG

CONTEXT OF INTEREST AND INQUIRY

THE SONG OF SONGS has always been enigmatic to me as a Latina Pente-costal in the United States. One reason for this is the long-standing taboo around the open discussion of erotic love in American Evangelical spaces, especially within Latinx congregations. This difficulty around the topic of sexual desire has led to a focus on allegorical interpretations of the book within these spaces. Yet, the allegorical interpretation of the Song of Songs was often regarded as being *too* colonially Catholic by *los evangélicos*.[1] As Latinx Pentecostals, we wanted to set ourselves apart from nominal Chris-tianity and cultural Catholicism as much as possible. This interpretive im-passe meant that the Song of Songs was often avoided altogether. From the pulpit or even in Sunday school, I rarely heard any passage from the Song of Songs mentioned. When queried, Sunday school teachers tried to explain that it was better to read the Song of Songs when I was older and married. Now that I am both, I have decided to examine the Song of Songs from within the milieu of my perspective as a Mexican American Pentecostal

1. Term for Protestant Evangelicals in Latin America.

biblical exegete, to highlight the prophetic female voice within the book as a vital contribution to the work of developing a more equal pulpit.

LATINX PENTECOSTAL HERMENEUTIC OF THE BIBLE

What characterizes a Latinx Pentecostal hermeneutic of the Bible is a focus on the *prophetic orthopathos* of Scripture. A prophetic orthopathos refers to a biblical exegete's invitation of the Holy Spirit to inspire solidarity with the divine pathos (suffering) so as to embody it as the prophets of the Old Testament did. Using this hermeneutic, the exegete focuses on how the authors and prophets of the biblical texts embody God's emotional engagement within creation. In other words, this reader of the Bible is interested in being angry about what God is angry about and being zealous for what God is zealous about. Samuel Solivan describes *orthopathos* as the "liberating appropriation of suffering."[2] This means acknowledging that the suffering of the disenfranchised at the hands of unjust systems *is* experienced by God in God's solidarity with the marginalized and his anger on their behalf. Furthermore, one cannot turn right doctrine into just practice without experiencing God's solidarity with the poor and marginalized. In Solivan's words, orthopathos is the "power of the Holy Spirit in one's life that transforms pathos, suffering and despair, into hope and wholeness."[3] Latinx hermeneutics can very well be a midwife in this endeavor. When one reads Scripture in community and in solidarity with the poor and marginalized, it opens us up to the testimony of Scripture that reveals the divine pathos concerning the disenfranchised.

Embracing the Negative Portrayal of Solomon's Identity in Scriptures via My Mestizaje

Coupled with this Latinx Pentecostal hermeneutic is my Mexican American Latina identity, at the core of which is an ownership of my *mestizaje*. *Mestizaje* refers the mixing of racial, ethnic, and cultural groups throughout Mexican history. Because I have owned that my cultural identity and ethnicity is a product of colonization, I recognize that I embody both the oppressor and oppressed. In embracing the paradox of my ethnocultural

2. Solivan, *Spirit, Pathos, and Liberation*, 11.
3. Solivan, *Spirit, Pathos, and Liberation*, 27.

identity, I have also developed the skill of embracing the conflicting portrayals of biblical characters and events. In the study of the Song of Songs, it is of the utmost importance to remember that the monarchy within the so-called Deuteronomistic History is portrayed both positively and negatively. As readers, we are cautioned to hold both portrayals in tension without rushing to harmonize them in order to understand the complexities of identity where no person (or culture/history containing the person depicted) is monolithic.

Solomon, the biblical character associated with the Song of Songs as well as the books of Proverbs and Qoheleth, is depicted both positively and negatively in 1 Kings 2:1—12:24. Rarely does scholarship fully embrace Solomon's dark side within the Former Prophets when interpreting his association with the Song of Songs. Instead, scholars choose to focus on the Bible's positive portrayal of Solomon (1 Kgs 2:1—9:14 and 10; cf. 2 Chr 1–9) when they look at Solomon's association with the books of Proverbs and Song of Songs. In this chapter, I will focus on the neglected negative depictions of Solomonic rulership within the Former Prophetic writings as the backdrop of Song of Songs 8 (1 Kgs 9:15–28;11:1—12:24).

The Prophetic Use of the Female Voice in Song of Songs

The female voice of the Song of Songs has been allegorically used to voice the church's desire for divine intimacy with their Creator for over two millennia. Although this is an important reading of the text, allegory alone restricts this piece of literature to the point that the literature loses its prophetic dimension—that is, when restricted by allegorical interpretations, the text loses its ability to speak on God's behalf for those who are marginalized in society. Although the gender of the book's author remains unknown, the Song of Songs presents with a concentrated use of the female voice. Even if, within the final form of this book, we discover that a male author or redactor has compiled this work, we must answer the question: What is the significance of the female voice in the author's conveyance of that person's message?

Jannie Hunter, in her essay titled "The Song of Protest: Reassessing the Song of Songs," proposes that the Song of Songs functions as protest literature within its first context(s) of ancient Israelite spaces. Hunter notes that the Song of Songs "stood in opposition to prevailing public morality as expressed and taught in the rest of the Old Testament," and that in the end, "the book's inclusion in the biblical canon may be a qualification of the Song of Songs as protest literature."[4] Hunter continues, "Regardless of the supposed Solomonic authorship, this protest aspect could have been a good reason to include the Song of Songs in the Canon."[5] I suggest that the book not only undermines traditional thought about Israelite sexuality; it also challenges the power structures of monarchy and the authoritative frameworks of patriarchy. In this way, the Song of Songs goes beyond protest and speaks in a prophetic voice. But is the prophetic voice a male voice or a female one?

The author of the Song of Songs uses both male and female voices to express their perspective within the author's context(s), but it is the female voice that is the dominant voice within the book. If one reads the Song of Songs as allegory *only*, one overlooks that between the voice of a Shulamite woman and the voices of females designated as the "daughters of Jerusalem," the book is dominated by a feminine perspective and voice. Furthermore, when reading the book allegorically, readers only focus on the love affair between the male and female in the book rather than on their cultural context and the systemic problems therein. Inversely, when the book is regarded as an edited compilation of erotic literature which underscores the female voice and is associated with the Solomonic kingdom, one must consider *more* than the eros expressed between the lovers; one must come to grips with why the lovers cannot come together openly within their cultural context under a Solomonic regime.

The best way to come to terms with the cultural power dynamics between the Shulamite, her family, and her lover (whether Solomon or not) is not by ignoring them, but by letting them inform the prophetic dimension of the text. The Shulamite is not only a woman but a woman of color who is outside of the ethnic bounds of Israel. On the other side, the female voice represents the collective women of the Israelite community, who are designated as daughters to their mother Jerusalem. The foreign female as well as of the daughters of Jerusalem are not merely given a voice; they are the embodiment of the prophetic voice itself.

Hunter proposes that the Song of Songs "presents itself as a song of protest in a society within which women are not allowed to speak openly on many matters where they desire to express an opinion."[6] Hunter says

4. Hunter, "The Song of Protest," 124.

5. Hunter, "The Song of Protest," 124.

6. Hunter, "The Song of Protest," 115.

that the Song of Songs is using the topic of love to "demonstrate about a central problem in society on behalf of those who suffer the most under the prevailing rules of that society."[7] It is the foreign woman on the outskirts of Israelite society and the women of Jerusalem under a Solomonic regime who experience the injustices that neglect of Torah creates among the people of God and their leaders. Leroy Waterman, explaining Solomon's role in the Song of Songs, suggests that even though Solomon is recalled as "Israel's most magnificent king," he was "also to the great contemporary body of Israelites the most hated ruler of their history." Waterman further clarifies why he believes Solomon is connected to the Song:

> It was true that he had held the spirit of the North in restraint for a time at Jerusalem, but it was not because of any affection on his part, but only for the purpose of gratifying his insatiable appetites and lusts. Yet the spirit of the North had never been broken, and their first love and loyalty had finally won them a reprieve that was like a release from the powers of the grave.[8]

Waterman concludes that even though the poem was not composed by Solomon, he should not be considered the lover of the Song of Songs; his role is as the "would-be destroyer of love" or as an anti-lover.[9]

In this type of prophetic reading of the text, the Song of Songs can be viewed as a critique of the Solomonic legacy within Israel. Starting with Solomon and continuing through the reigns of his successors Rehoboam and Jeroboam I, the monarchy has been linked to both idolatry and injustice against marginalized members of society. In this chapter, we will look at Song of Songs chapter 8 as a case study of the feminine voice, which nests within a patriarchal literary perspective, and what this voice accomplishes in informing and limiting the message of Scripture.

EXEGETICAL ANALYSIS OF THE TEXT: SONG OF SONGS 8

The speaker desires a deep intimacy with the addressee, one that is expressed as a desire for kinship (Song 8:1a). In previous chapters, the male lover uses kinship language to express the intimacy between himself and

7. Hunter, "The Song of Protest," 115.

8. Waterman, "The Rôle of Solomon in the Song of Songs," 184.

9. Waterman, "The Rôle of Solomon in the Song of Songs," 184.

the female lover (Song 8:1, 2, 8–10), but it is clearly stated in the rest of the book that the female lover is a foreigner, a Shulamite (Song 4:1–15; 6:9, 13). That this foreign speaker expresses that she would like to display affection for her beloved in this context demonstrates that the speaker would settle for at least the level of intimacy that being in her beloved's ethnic group could afford her.

Motherhood and the marital bed overlap thematically where the speaker's nursing mother is used to draw the addressee closer to the speaker (Song 8:1b). The rationale for this desire for intimacy is expressed in the second couplet (8:1c–d). Cynthia R. Chapman suggests that the use of the word pair "house of my mother" in v. 2 is best understood as an instance of practiced "nesting matriarchy" within the patriarchal ideal of dominant culture.[10] The speaker craves the ability to openly kiss the addressee without fear of being despised by society (8:1c–d). The "house of the mother" connotes a level of matriarchal power and authority in the realm of appropriate affection between men and women within the kinship group (8:2a–b). It was common in this ancient Near Eastern culture to express ethnic kinship through the sharing of wet-nurses between what were called "milk siblings." It is within this kinship group that physical affection and intimacy could be displayed between members of the opposite sex without the stigma of being sexualized or viewed as incestuous.[11]

There is a significant shift from the speaker's desire for kinship and acceptable public display of affection within the realm of the "house of her mother" (i.e., ethnic grouping, 8:1–2b) to a desire for a private and sexual encounter in the inner and lockable chamber of her mother's house (heder hôratî, 8:2c).[12] It is in this inner room where the speaker provides spiced wine to her beloved (8:2d–e). The idea that the speaker would like to sexualize their relationship in this last portion of the book is furthered by the next verse where the speaker declares a longing to be held in a passionate manner with her beloved's left hand under her head and his right hand embracing her (8:3). The daughters of Jerusalem are warned against awakening love before it is appropriate (8:4).

The next verse conveys a question that appears to be a response from the collective group of women from the previous verse. The daughters of Jerusalem ask who the woman is who is coming up from the wilderness

10. Chapman, The House of the Mother, 29.

11. Chapman, The House of the Mother, 15.

12. Chapman, The House of the Mother, 77.

leaning upon her beloved (8:5a–b). To that question another female voice responds, not to the group of women, but now to the beloved. It is unclear if her beloved is with another woman and the daughters of Jerusalem are making the speaker aware of it, or if the question posed by the daughters of Jerusalem is meant to be understood rhetorically to serve as an acknowledgment that the speaker has addressed them. What is clear is that the single female speaker does not answer the women's question but instead addresses the male beloved singularly. She does so by saying that she awakened her beloved under an apple tree (8:5c). In the last couplet of v. 5, the speaker pays homage to her beloved's mother as the source of her beloved's existence by speaking of the place under the apple tree as being her beloved's place of origin. These lines accentuate what the speaker has exclaimed in v. 1, that she is a foreigner.

Moving from speaking of the origin of her beloved's life, the speaker turns to speak of love as something comparable to death (8:6). The speaker demands that her beloved place her as a seal upon his heart and as a seal upon his forearm (8:6a–b). In her article "Lovely Wordplay in Canticles 8,6a," Valerie Kabergs says that the "request of the woman to be set 'as a seal' upon her lover's heart thus symbolizes her longing for a shared identity."[13] Kabergs also suggests that "in asking to be set upon her lover's heart as a seal, the woman requests that the heart of the man would be »sealed« against every other woman" and that this "longing for exclusivity is strengthened by the use of the noun קנאה ("jealousy") in Cant 8,6b."[14] According to Kabergs, this is one interpretation of the wordplay, but there are two possibilities:

> As both the literal and the metaphorical meaning of the noun זרוע are frequently attested in the Hebrew Bible, it is plausible that the phrase in Cant 8,6a could be interpreted in two—both legitimate, yet alternative—ways: 1) "set me as a seal upon your *arm*" or 2) "take me to heart as a seal upon your *strength*." In her request to be "taken to heart" in Cant 8,6a the woman expects her lover to have her in mind, to consider and care for her. She does not beg desperately for love, but instead strongly *advises* the male *person* to acknowledge her love to be his strength.[15]

13. Kabergs, "Lovely Wordplay in Canticles 8,6a," 262.
14. Kabergs, "Lovely Wordplay," 263.
15. Kabergs, "Lovely Wordplay," 263.

The reason that the speaker gives is that love is as strong as death, and jealousy is as fierce as the grave (8:6c–d).[16] This couplet appears to say that the woman who is leaning on her beloved is another woman and not the speaker herself. If this is the case, then the last couplet of v. 6 makes sense as describing the intense anger that she now has in seeing her beloved with another woman (8:6e–f). The speaker is inflamed with anger. In her article titled "Green-Eyed Lovers: A Study of Jealousy in Song of Songs 8:5–7," Havilah Dharamraj interprets the jealousy of the woman as a remarkable feature of the Song of Songs because it portrays a woman who is (just) as jealous as any male in the Old Testament. Dharamraj also notes that the only other biblical character that voices this type of anger and jealousy over issues of exclusivity is the God of the exodus.[17] The next verse assures the beloved male that the speaker's love is unquenchable, and that she understands that this love comes with a price—that if a man were to offer his lover the wealth of his house rather than returning her love, he would be held in contempt (8:7). Perhaps the speaker is acknowledging that in order for her to be with her beloved, the beloved would have to give up his privilege, wealth, and status.

The daughters of Jerusalem come back to express concern for protecting their prepubescent "little sister" before she is betrothed (8:8). The little girl's age is indicated by her lack of breasts. This would suggest that, unlike the lactating mother of v. 1 or the mother figure who gives birth to the beloved in v. 5, this little sister has no house or voice of her own; instead, she must be "spoken for." The daughters of Jerusalem answer their own question in v. 9 with two conditional statements describing two distinct scenarios with corresponding apodoses (main clauses) where the speakers respond accordingly. If the little sister is a wall (that is to say, if she is impenetrable), then the daughters of Jerusalem will reinforce her safety with a battlement of silver (8:8a–b). If the little sister can be opened like a door (that is to say, if she is vulnerable), then the daughters of Jerusalem will board her up to make her into a wall (8:9c–d). The original female speaker answers the daughters of Jerusalem by lamenting that she was once a wall. When she was a wall, her breasts served her like towers of refuge for her

---

16. Aren Wilson-Wright argues that love in this poem is portrayed like Yahweh who defeats chaotic waters since "Song 8:6b–7a identifies love with the victorious divine warrior. Like YHWH and Baal, love tangles with Death and Sea and proves an equal match for both opponents" (Wilson-Wright, "Love Conquers All," 343).

17. Havilah, "Green-Eyed Lovers."

beloved, who found peace within her (8:10). The speaker is turning the image of the wall used by the daughters of Jerusalem on its head.

Cheryl Exum, Elaine James, and Scott Spencer all agree that the female lover is the speaker in 8:8.[18] Exum builds a good argument first for understanding this as the female lover's voice quoting her brothers. Although I do agree that this is a female voice and not that of male characters not within the text, I assign the voice to the daughters of Jerusalem since 8:8 is written in the first common plural. Since the daughters of Jerusalem have already started a conversation with the female lover, I see no reason why they are silenced after their initial question in 8:5. I do not think that the brothers of the female lover are being quoted by the singular female as one of their taunts. Within my view, this is reading too much into the text. Exum is correct when she understands Song 8:8–14 as a dialogue, but she views it as between the two lovers.[19] Instead, I understand this as an exchange between the female lover and the daughters of Jerusalem since the male lover is introduced in the poem as the one being observed and as one to whom the female lover speaks from a distance. It is not until v. 13, that readers are clear that the male lover has returned to address the female lover directly.

The daughters of Jerusalem shift from speaking about their sister to now speaking about Solomon in v. 11. They praise Solomon's vineyard that he entrusted to keepers who made a profit of a thousand pieces of silver each for its fruit. I suggest that v. 11 foregrounds the collective voice of a group of women because it would fit a pattern of the daughters of Jerusalem describing a single figure and the initial speaker responding to them with some self-disclosure about the topic of which they speak. This pattern starts in vv. 5–7 and, within my view, continues in vv. 8–10. This pattern is repeated here in vv. 11–12, where the subject is not the little sister, but King Solomon who capitalizes upon the fruit of his vineyard by charging a thousand pieces of silver for it (8:11).

The location of Solomon's vineyard is called Baal-hamon and is only mentioned once in the Hebrew Bible. It is unclear if this is an actual vineyard with either hired tenant farmers or slaves who were of the Shulamite's kinship group located in Lebanon (Song 1:4; 4:8) or if the vineyard is a metaphor for Solomon's harem.[20] Either way, the place itself is named after

18 Exum, "The Little Sister and Solomon's Vineyard"; James, "A City Who Surrenders"; Spencer, "Feeling the Burn."

19. Exum, "The Little Sister and Solomon's Vineyard," 281–82.

20. McGinniss, "'What Is He Doing in That Book?'"

the Canaanite deity Baal and is historically linked to a type of exploitation. If the vineyard is entrusted to keepers by Solomon, one would venture to ask the question whether or not this labor is another example of the slave labor Solomon was notorious for in 1 Kings 9:20–21; 12:4–14. If this is not a literal vineyard, one can look to the rest of the book for clues as to how the author uses botanical language in reference to female sexuality (4:12, 16; 5:1; 7:12). In either case, whether slave labor increases Solomon's wealth or female sexuality is being monetized under his regime, v. 11 does not cast a completely positive light upon the figure Solomon.

In response to the daughters of Jerusalem, the Shulamite claims ownership of her own vineyard since her beloved, acting like Solomon, has seemingly turned his attention to another woman (8:12).[21] An alternate reading would be that one of the keepers reclaims ownership of his vineyard. Although this reading corroborates the understanding of the vineyard of v. 11 as a literal plot of land used for cultivation, within a literary context, the speaker appears to be the initial speaker, the Shulamite, since the one who responds to her in v. 13 identifies the prior speaker as singular and female.

Because of this, I understand that in v. 12, the female who starts this poem in this chapter is the one who is reclaiming ownership of her vineyard. This woman takes back her land or sexuality as her own (8:12a). In doing so, she challenges the Solomonic regime directly (8:12b). In contrast to her one vineyard, Solomon has the thousand silver pieces and two hundred keepers of fruit (8:12b–c). Exum is not convinced that Solomon would be "the butt of a joke or the object of criticism here" since to Exum, "King Solomon is portrayed positively (3:6–11) and the man assumes a royal guise as 'the king' (1:4, 12; 7:6[5])." Based on their language, all the passages that Exum cites are not necessarily positive portrayals of the Solomonic monarchy; they are merely calls to look at Solomon's wealth. There are no positive or negative judgments passed on portrayals of Solomon until chapter 8.[22]

Breaking the pattern of most of the chapter, the male beloved's voice responds to the Shulamite one last time (8:13). He identifies his addressee as the singular female voice. He calls her the one who dwells in the gardens (8:13a). He warns her that his guildsmen are listening for her voice (8:13b), but that he wishes to hear her voice himself (8:13c). Given that

---

21. Tremper Longman's view is that the lovers' relationship is contrasted with Solomon's polygamy here in v. 12 (Longman, *Song of Songs*, 220).

22. Exum, "The Little Sister and Solomon's Vineyard," 279.

the Shulamite was beaten by the king's watchmen in prior chapters when she was looking for her beloved (5:7), I am categorizing the beloved male's words as a warning to the Shulamite that he wants to be the first to hear her voice *before* his companions can hear her (8:13b–c). In response, the Shulamite renews her faith in her beloved and entreats him to hurry to her rescue (8:14). There is hope for their love to be renewed, albeit within an oppressive and demoralizing context. The main question of the poem is whether the couple's relationship is appropriate. Given the context of their relationship, the likelihood that the couple from the Song of Songs will find wedded bliss appears limited.

CONCLUSION

The female (Shulamite) voice expresses a longing for ethnic inclusion, relational acceptance, and sexual intimacy. With this expression of her devotion to Solomon come declarations of jealousy, regret, anger, and self-possession for the duration of the poem. Perhaps the prophetic voice could best express itself in the female voice. This self-aware and daring female appears to become a damsel in distress when she utters the last line of the book. Her portrayal as a complex character is seemingly undermined by the last verse assigned to her at the end of the poem, but is this so? The male lover *also* appears to be captive to this oppressive Solomonic regime where he has to sneak away to be with the Shulamite and is unable to control the actions of his men in relation to his lover. If there is a legitimate female voice, it is undermined by the monarchical and patriarchal systems that confine all people regardless of gender.

The Shulamite's voice is most effective in speaking prophetically in this context to the figure of Solomon. It is ironic that a foreign woman would be used to critique a king who turned his heart away from God because of his foreign wives. When one looks at the female's voice in Song of Songs 8 as a prophetic voice, she embodies the divine pathos. In this embodiment, the Shulamite's identity informs readers of how God is in solidarity with her disenfranchisement within the story of the book. The female's desire for exclusivity, her jealousy, and even her rage then voice the jealousy and wrath of God himself against the idolatry and injustice that characterizes Solomon's legacy in both Israel and Judah. The female's identity as a foreigner and as a fieldworker shows the intersectional nature of the injustices experienced under a Solomonic regime. Her longing for intimacy with her lover becomes more than sexual desire. It is a cry for inclusion within socioethnic spheres.

Implications for a More Equal Pulpit

Just as the Shulamite's voice embodies the divine pathos prophetically, so do the female voices within our congregations. God's Spirit will speak through those who are being silenced in our churches, and this begins with the female voice, which has been silenced the most in our places of worship. When we listen to the female voice from our pulpits, we invite the divine pathos of compassion to be performed and embodied prophetically. When both men and women preach and embody God's word to a congregation, this adds a different dimension to a congregation, where all are welcomed and included. This welcome and inclusion are not just for women but also for men who suffer injustice because of racial, ethnic, ableist, socioeconomic, or any other type of exclusion. Surely, female voices are not the only voices that are silenced within our churches, but the female voice speaks prophetically to the divine pathos in such a way that the message gives way to a more equal pulpit.

IMPLICATIONS FOR TODAY'S PULPIT:

1. How does the gendered voice of a speaker inform and sometimes embody the message of the speaker?

2. Does gendered language matter in relaying a message to the people of God? What does gendered language accomplish in preaching?

3. Must a speaker always be male in order for the word of God to be preached? Why would the author of Song of Songs give voice to the Shulmanite woman given her intersectional situation in society?

4. How can the Song of Songs inform how the church gives voice to multiple speakers within the congregation?

BIBLIOGRAPHY

Alden, Robert L. "Song of Songs 8:12a: Who Said It?" *Journal of the Evangelical Theological Society* 31 (1988) 269–78.

Alegre Heitzmann, Alfonso. "El Cantar de Los Cantares: Poesía y Ritual de La Pascua." *Estudios Bíblicos* 43/3–4 (1985) 321–30.

Brenner, Athalya, and Carole R. Fontaine, eds. *A Feminist Companion to Song of Songs.* The Feminist Companion to the Bible 2nd ser. 6. Sheffield: Sheffield Academic, 2000.

Charry, Ellen T. "Female Sexuality as an Image of Empowerment: Two Models." *Saint Luke's Journal of Theology* 30 (1987) 201–18.

Chapman, Cynthia R. *The House of the Mother: The Social Roles of Maternal Kin in Biblical Hebrew Narrative and Poetry.* New Haven: Yale University Press, 2016.

Dharamraj, Havilah. "Green-Eyed Lovers: A Study of Jealousy in Song of Songs 8:5–7." *Priscilla Papers* 32.1 (2018) 3–8.

Exum, J. Cheryl. "The Little Sister and Solomon's Vineyard: Song of Songs 8:8–12 as a Lovers' Dialogue." In *Seeking Out the Wisdom of the Ancients: Essays Offered to Honor Michael V. Fox on the Occasion of His Sixty-fifth Birthday*, edited by Ronald L. Troxel et al., 269–82. Winona Lake, IN: Eisenbrauns, 2005.

Gault, Brian P. "An Admonition against 'Rousing Love': The Meaning of the Enigmatic Refrain in Song of Songs." *Bulletin for Biblical Research* 20/2 (2010) 161–84.

Hess, Richard S. *Song of Songs.* Baker Commentary on the Old Testament. Wisdom and Psalms. Grand Rapids: Baker Academic, 2005.

Hunter, Jannie H. "The Song of Protest: Reassessing the Song of Songs." *Journal for the Study of the Old Testament* 25/90 (2000) 109–24.

James, Elaine Theresa. "A City Who Surrenders: Song 8:8–10." *Vetus Testamentum* 67 (2017) 448–57.

Jenson, Robert W. *Song of Songs.* Interpretation. Louisville: John Knox, 2005.

Kabergs, Valérie. "Lovely Wordplay in Canticles 8,6a." *Zeitschrift für die Alttestamentliche Wissenschaft* 126 (2014) 261–64.

Longman, Tremper. *Song of Songs.* New International Commentary on the Old Testament. Grand Rapids: Eerdmans, 2001.

McGinniss, Mark. "'What Is He Doing in That Book?' Solomon's Role in the Song of Songs." *Journal of Ministry and Theology* 12/2 (2008) 84–106.

Murphy, Roland E. *The Song of Songs: A Commentary on the Book of Canticles or the Song of Songs.* Hermeneia. Minneapolis: Fortress, 1990.

Pope, Marvin H. *Song of Songs.* Anchor Bible 7C. Garden City, NY: Doubleday, 1977.

Spencer, F. Scott "The Beautiful Black Woman in Song of Songs—Her Too!" *The Bible Today* 57.3 (2019) 150–56.

———. "Feeling the Burn: Angry Brothers, Adamant Sister, and Affective Relations in the Song of Songs (1:5–6; 8:8–12)." *Catholic Biblical Quarterly* 81 (2019) 405–28.

Waterman, Leroy. "The Rôle of Solomon in the Song of Songs." *Journal of Biblical Literature* 44 (1925) 171–87.

Watson, Wilfred G. E. "Love and Death Once More (Song of Songs VIII 6)." *Vetus Testamentum* 47 (1997) 385–87.

Wilson-Wright, Aren. "Love Conquers All: Song of Songs 8:6b–7a as a Reflex of the Northwest Semitic Combat Myth." *Journal of Biblical Literature* 134 (2015) 333–45.

5

Pulling Up a Seat at the Leader's Table

JANETTE H. OK

SOCIAL LOCATION AND SPACE MAKING

WHEN I THINK ABOUT my formation as a pastor, preacher, and scholar, I trace my journey along significant mentors who have indelibly impacted my imagination, vision, and sense of vocation for leadership in the church. The first of these was my mother. While I didn't truly appreciate what a trailblazing, powerhouse of a woman she was until I grew older, I had my suspicions. Mom never spoke of what roles belong to women and which belong to men. Instead, she expected excellence and great things from *both* me and my brother. She modeled for me that I don't have to choose between motherhood and a career. As a woman, she did not shy away from leadership within the church; and as an immigrant, she did not shy away from being involved in the community and vocal at the workplace.

It was my mother, along with my father, who introduced me to the Korean American church and to my Christian faith. The Korean church that my family and I attended in Michigan made the very significant but unconventional decision to hire a Korean American female pastor to lead its young adult English Ministry (EM)—this was over thirty years ago! Even though I was just a kid at the time, my mom would take me to these EM services so I could hear the Reverend Mary Paik preach. I vividly remember this young minister speaking with such authority, grace, and power and sending us off each week with the benediction. I clung to this memory during the drought of exposure to female preachers that I experienced for years afterwards. Mary cleared a path for the trajectory of my life to take shape. Her example—the fact that she even exists and pastored faithfully for years—gave me tangible evidence that despite what people said to the contrary, women could and should preach and pastor. So my formation as a pastor and a preacher began when as a little girl, I witnessed firsthand a woman pastor who embodied what a leader looks like and expanded my imagination.

My identity as a leader continued to grow in the summer before sixth grade. First, at a weeklong overnight camp for Korean American youth at the Sae Jong Camp, in Michigan, I received an award at the end of the week. The award read, "Janette is bound to become a Sae Jong camp counselor someday due to her leadership abilities." That was the first time I saw myself a leader, and ever since I have tried to discover what it meant to be a great one. It was also during this same summer that I experienced my new birth and became a follower of Jesus. I realized that my salvation in Christ wasn't something I could earn or achieve but a gift of sheer grace for me to receive and live into.

It was during this time that my family moved to California where we attended a church that fostered my love for God and God's word. But it was also at this church where I experienced the rude awakening that my experience of seeing an ordained woman pastor was not the norm but the exception. I was a freshman in high school. During a church retreat, I naively shared with a retreat speaker that I wanted to become a pastor. Surprised and troubled, he told me, "God used women like Deborah to lead his people only when he could not find faithful men to rise to the challenge." Now, I didn't know who Deborah was at the time and had never learned from the book of Judges save for hearing stories about Samson. So, this pastor had me flummoxed. But let me tell you, after I left that meeting, I was determined to study the Bible for myself. And I should note, while there were many discouragements and setbacks along the way, I have since had the all too rare but formative experience of being a member of churches that entrusted me with opportunities to serve not only behind the scenes but in official leadership capacities, including in the pulpit.

Along the way, I've had several important teachers come into my life. At UCLA, it was professor Scott Bartchy, whose lectures on the historical Jesus and early Christianity rocked my world. He is the reason I became a biblical scholar. It was in his classes and during our conversations that I discovered my love for the New Testament and its community-shaping, relationship-transforming, and behavior-altering ethic. I took every one of his classes and did my senior thesis under his supervision. Scott helped me discover how my love for the church and biblical scholarship could intersect. At Princeton Theological Seminary, I met Dr. Brian Blount, who helped me imagine the possibility of having a bivocational calling as a pastor and a scholar. From him I learned how to teach like a preacher and to preach like a teacher. His scholarship reflects the African American ministry context from which he pastored for many years. His preaching and teaching bridge the world of academia and the needs and realities of the local church. Brian taught me to read biblical texts carefully and exegetically, but to also take my own context and that of my community seriously. Though never one of my professors, another of my significant mentors, and fellow contributor to this book, is Dr. Gale Yee. From Gale I learned the importance of mentorship, collegiality, sisterhood, and bringing others along for the journey. She has mentored countless students and scholars in biblical studies. Her commitment to investing in Asian and Asian American women in theology and ministry has influenced multiple generations of leaders. Gale reminds me that our work isn't just about our work but about the communities it helps form and the lives it impacts for the kingdom of God.

As a teacher, the experiences and the challenges I faced in my own journey as a second-generation Korean American female pastor and biblical scholar, wife, and mother have shaped my pedagogical approaches and the importance I place on exposing my students to diverse voices. They have also impacted my pastoral ministry and the weight I place on investing in Christian leaders who are humble, courageous, full of integrity, and collaborative—embodying and proclaiming the gospel of grace and justice. My social location as a Korean American Christian woman is not only rooted in my identity and positionality, but also in the relationships and communities that have helped form me and make space for me.

In ministry, I have had the all too rare but formative experience of serving in churches that have entrusted me with opportunities not only behind the scenes but in official leadership capacities, including preaching in the pulpit. The strong support and encouragement from both men and women has helped me endure the discouragement, frustration, and sexism (overt and covert) that women too often face. One particular brother who has empowered me is my senior pastor and colleague, Pastor Bryan Kim. Years before Ekko Church was founded, Bryan and I would talk ministry and commiserate about our experiences and struggles as young pastors at our respective churches. We dreamed with our spouses about planting a church together—what would be its values and who it would serve? Bryan was the first male Asian American pastor who asked me for advice (I mean, a lot of advice!), and who acknowledged that some of his most influential mentors in ministry were women. He advocated and created the pathway for me to become the first pastor ordained by our church. He also convinced me, despite my reservations, and trusted me to serve as acting lead pastor during his sabbatical. At Ekko Church, I am privileged to be a part of a growing pastoral team and to serve alongside a visionary leader who believes that shared leadership among women and men better serves the kingdom of God.

PULLING UP A SEAT AT THE TABLE: LUKE 10:38–42[1]

The call to ministry is a call to leadership, but all too often, women struggle to fulfill this call. On the one hand, I find that women in particular tend to shy away from embracing and embodying the fact that they are leaders. This is in conjunction with our surrounding systems and structures that actively obstruct us from the opportunities to do so. I joke that it is much easier for a camel to go through the eye of a needle than a woman to have the opportunity to lead a church as a preacher and pastor.

To illuminate this situation, I look to a passage that many of us may be familiar with, the story of Martha and Mary found in Luke 10:38–42. As we study this passage, pay attention to Mary's remarkable display of courage as an example for many of us women of how we can enter spaces of leadership. Also notice Jesus's gracious response to Mary's bold act as an example for

---

1. The contents of this section were originally presented at the Sider Institute's Empowering Women in Ministry Conference held on October 11, 2019, at Grantham Church on the campus of Messiah College in Mechanicsburg, Pennsylvania. It was later published under the title, "Leading with Imagination: How to Cultivate Women Leaders in Our Churches" in *Brethren in Christ History & Life* 43.1 (2020) 70–79. I would like to thank the journal's editor, Harriett Bicksler, for granting me permission to republish the article here. Please note that some of the content has been revised.

those of us in positions of authority of how we can make space for women leaders.

> 38 Now as they went on their way, he entered a certain village, where a woman named Martha welcomed him into her home. 39 She had a sister named Mary, who sat at the Lord's feet and listened to what he was saying. 40 But Martha was distracted by her many tasks; so she came to him and asked, "Lord, do you not care that my sister has left me to do all the work by myself? Tell her then to help me." 41 But the Lord answered her, "Martha, Martha, you are worried and distracted by many things; 42 there is need of only one thing. Mary has chosen the better part, which will not be taken away from her." (Luke 10:38–42)

Contrary to the ways this passage has been interpreted to pit one sister against the other, I believe Luke holds both women up as exemplary disciples. Martha "welcomes" (*hupodechomai*) Jesus into her home not only as an attentive host but as a devoted, albeit distracted, disciple. Meanwhile, Mary "listens" (*akouō*) at the feet of Jesus not as a negligent host but as an attentive and assertive disciple.[2] Now we don't know for sure if Martha is the eldest sister, but we certainly get the impression that she is a leader in the house. Martha's hospitable reception of Jesus contrasts the lack of reception by a Samaritan village in 9:51–53: "When the days drew near for him to be taken up, he set his face to go to Jerusalem. And he sent messengers ahead of him. On their way they entered a village of the Samaritans to make ready for him; but they did not receive him, because his face was set toward Jerusalem."

Earlier in Luke 10:4–9, Jesus's instructions to the seventy reveal how the hospitality of strangers is essential to the work and ministry of Jesus and his travel companions: "Carry no purse, no bag, no sandals; and greet no one on the road. Whatever house you enter, first say, 'Peace to this house!' . . . Remain in the same house, eating and drinking whatever they provide . . . Whenever you enter a town and its people welcome you, eat what is set before you; cure the sick who are there, and say to them, 'The kingdom of God has come near to you.'" By receiving Jesus into her home, Martha embraces both Jesus and his mission. The practice of hospitality in the ancient Mediterranean world was a fundamental and sacred custom. As

2. Mary and Martha also figure prominently in John's Gospel but always in relation to Lazarus their brother. In John 12:1, Jesus enters the home of Lazarus. Luke, however, makes no mention of Lazarus and tells us that Jesus enters the home of Martha (10:38). Martha serves as host to Jesus and his companions.

an itinerant preacher, Jesus moved with the twelve disciples from place to place and relied on the hospitality of others. Martha behaves appropriately, graciously, and generously. In this sense, it is Mary who fails to pull her weight. Mary is supposed to be Martha's wing-woman, but instead she abdicates her responsibility by sitting at Jesus' feet. Who does Mary think she is? Why does Jesus admonish Martha, not Mary?

Though the text does indicate exactly what tasks or work preoccupy Martha, I think it is safe to assume that she acts out of love for Jesus. Interestingly, Jesus does not reprimand Martha for being busy with her many *diakonia* (or "tasks" as the NRSV translates it in v. 40). It is not until Martha complains about her work and her sister's unhelpfulness that Jesus says, "Martha, Martha, you are worried and distracted by many things" (10:41). The repetition of her name is an expression of his tender affection, not gruff agitation.[3] It's as if Jesus sees her outer flurry and addresses the state of her heart. He doesn't just notice Martha, but he knows her and sees her, just as he does Mary.

On the other hand, Mary is not being passive when she positions herself at the feet of Jesus. Rather, she does the equivalent of pulling up a seat at the table normally occupied by male disciples (cf. Acts 22:3). Mary boldly asserts her discipleship by insisting, through her act of sitting, that traditional gender roles do not disqualify her from listening to Jesus's word.[4] She apparently has a habit of breaking with conventions when it comes to being around Jesus' feet! In John, Mary commits the flagrant act of anointing Jesus' feet with costly perfume and wiping them with her hair (12:3). In both cases, Mary sits at Jesus' feet as his servant, disciple, and worshipper, and Jesus affirms her. I think he would do the same for Martha if she would sit and receive from him. I imagine him saying, "Rather than be so concerned with what's *on* the table, Martha, please take a seat *at* the table next to Mary and the other disciples."

Now to be clear, a life of discipleship isn't simply a life of adoration, contemplation, and sitting. (And remember, Mary didn't stay at Jesus' feet indefinitely! Also, we don't know how the story ends, but maybe Martha decides to join her sister and also pull up a seat at the table, so to speak.) Jesus' disciples performed signs and wonders and great acts of service. They

3. Cf. Luke 13:34; 22:31.

4. The verb *akouō* used to describe Mary's listening is the same word used by Jesus when he replies to woman's praise, "Blessed is the womb that bore you and the breasts the nursed you!" with the correction, "Blessed rather are those who hear the word of God and obey it!" (Luke 11:27–28).

preached the gospel even in the face of opposition and persecution. They waited on tables, took care of widows, and planted and pastored churches. Jesus is not saying that Martha's activity and service are wrong. The fact that the parable of the good Samaritan (10:25–36) immediately precedes this story only underscores this point. It is the Samaritan—the social and religious outcast—whose actions reflect the neighborly love God desires of his people, but it is Mary—the woman who is supposed to serve the men in the room—whose actions reflect the posture and devotion God also desires of his people. The juxtaposition of Jesus' positive evaluation of both the Samaritan man and Mary puts in sharper relief the way radical love and discipleship in the kingdom of God are embodied and modeled by those Luke's readers would least expect.

So, what makes Mary's choice to sit at Jesus' feet and listen to Jesus' words in this situation better than Martha's choice to perform many tasks on his behalf (with great love, no doubt)? Mary, I think, recognizes that *being* with Jesus takes precedence over *doing* things for Jesus. This is why she has chosen the better part, which in Greek is literally "good portion" (Luke 10:42). We cannot say we love God without loving our neighbor. Participation in God's salvific story for humanity requires compassionate, risky, boundary-breaking action. But in order to participate fully in this story, we need to sit in the presence of Jesus, who fulfills it. To sit and listen is risky and countercultural, is it not? It's hard—especially for many women disciples and leaders—to be on the receiving end of ministry. We give, we impart, we intercede, and we serve. But do we receive? Do we sit? Do we delight?

Where do we sit or stand in this story? And how do we envision Jesus responding to our acts of doing or being?

One of the hardest things I had to get used to as a young woman leader was entering into conversations and spaces where I didn't always feel welcome. The call to pastoral ministry is a call to servant leadership. I knew I needed to dig my hands in the dirt of service, but I also wanted to engage in conversations about ministry and gain experience in the pulpit. I also learned from observation and experience that women who intentionally sought to develop their leadership gifts and find their voice through practice and mentorship were often misconstrued as power hungry. As a twenty-year-old college student, children's pastor, and aspiring seminarian, I wanted a piece of the action at the table and to have opportunities to preach in the pulpit, not to acquire more power for myself, but to faithfully use my influence and gifts to serve others. How does one do this?

STEPS TOWARDS A MORE EQUAL PULPIT

Here are some suggestions for how to get in the posture of leadership and create pathways for future leaders in our churches:

1. Pull up a chair and sit at the table.

- Sisters, when you're in a meeting or gathering full of men, resist the urge to occupy the corners of the room or to be as invisible as possible. Pull up a chair, sit at the table or wherever the action is, and participate in the conversation.

- Be aware of how you lead with your bodies. Leaders embody space and are sensitive to how they use their bodies, physical gestures, speech, and influence. MaryKate Morse, in her excellent book *Making Room for Leadership*, explains that "true leadership happens between the lines, in the interpersonal relational processes in social settings . . . it's how you enter a room, position yourself to speak, modulate your face and use your eyes, while at the same time assessing others who are sharing the same space."[5]

- The same is true for those in positions of authority. Pay attention to how you embody your power. Some of us need to take up less space. Some of us need to take up more. Some of us need to learn how to adapt our use of space by taking up less or more depending on the situation. Do not underestimate the impact of the way you speak, gesture, give or avoid eye contact, stand or sit, etc., on others. Jesus embodied his authority in ways that drew the sick, marginalized, unclean, sinful, and broken to him and empowered them to go in faith and peace (e.g., Luke 7:36–50; 8:26–39; 8:43–48).

- Too often, leaders with official titles and positions assume that if emerging or potential leaders want to join the table, they'll simply pull up a chair and participate. But this is not often the case. Be intentional about making space and inviting others to the table, especially women and people of color. Be aware of how even physical

5. Morse, *Making Room for Leadership*, 25.

table and seating arrangements can marginalize certain people and focus the center of gravity on others.

2. Seek Mentors.

- Rather than wait for the mentors to come to you, seek them out. But be generous and flexible with the idea of a mentor and open to finding mentors in unexpected places. I haven't personally met some of my mentors, and some of them have been dead for years! I've met mentors in books and through podcasts and online sermons. Be a student of leaders, pastors, preachers, and teachers whom you admire and who differ from you. Listen to their talks, sermons, and lectures. Read their books. These guides don't have to be your official "mentor" in order to teach you.

- If and when you do have opportunity to meet in person with someone whom you want to learn from, make it easy for them to invest in you by being teachable and considerate. Be on time for your meetings, offer to buy coffee, be ready with focused questions, jot down notes, and consider following up with a thank-you card or email.

3. Be a mentor to women.

- Invite prospective male *and* female seminarians out to lunch. Take both male *and* female interns to conferences where you speak and to meetings with other leaders. Don't obstruct pathways for the development of women leaders by making women out to be liabilities for men in ministry and by keeping women out of the room. Mentoring is about sharing power, not holding power or abusing it, and thus requires accountability, caution, and of course, wisdom.

- If you see a young woman in your church brimming with ministry-related and theological and biblical questions and who is gifted and passionate about serving the church, ask her about her dreams for how she might serve God and just listen. Tell her you see gifts in her. Talk to her about seminary. Connect her to resources and other possible mentors.

4. Invest financially in women leaders.

- Create a seminary scholarship fund. A seminary education is never wasted on the church. And while seminary does not a pastor make, women with pastoral gifts benefit from being encouraged and financially supported to go to seminary, as do the churches who develop and hire them.

- Establish fair and flexible parental leave policies. This is vital to promoting fair and shared leadership and giving women real options for "staying in the game" even while raising young children. When churches offer parental leave for both mothers and fathers, it encourages more equal partnership in parenting and disrupts the false notion that a woman cannot pastor and mother at the same time.

5. Be in solidarity—not competition—with other women.

- Sisters, support and celebrate the growth, success, and achievements of other women. Share in one another's struggles, challenges, and frustrations. Honor the women who have come before you and invest in and mentor women who come after you. We're in this together!

- Brothers, this goes for you, too. We need your solidarity, support, advocacy, and collaboration.

- Invite female preachers to speak not only to women and at women's retreats but on Sundays, as keynote speakers, and at churchwide retreats where men and women are both present.

- Read, quote, and cite women, including female scholars, leaders, and pastors. Show your congregation that you are shaped and taught by women theologians, biblical scholars, thinkers, and ministers. Celebrate the fact that you too are discipled and equipped by women (including mothers, grandmothers, teachers, neighbors) and talk about them.

- If you haven't done so already, make friends with women in ministry. You need women colleagues from whom you're willing to learn, to whom you're willing to listen, and with whom you can collaborate and cast a vision. The lack of gender diversity on any pastoral team or ministry staff stunts the imagination and creative potential for dynamic models of leadership in our congregations.

- Avoid setting up events or conferences where all the speakers are male. You'll be able to do this when you actually develop ongoing relationships with women and people of color who are your friends and colleagues in ministry. Don't simply incorporate women into your events as a way to include their presence, but do so to also challenge patriarchy and sexist structures and ways of thinking.

6. Train yourself to not say sorry so much.

- Sisters, don't apologize for having an opinion, asking questions, or wanting to learn. Avoid beginning your sentences with disqualifiers like "This may be a stupid question, but . . ." Or starting a talk or sermon by shooting yourself in the foot with "I'm so nervous because I don't usually speak in front of people." Avoid concluding your sentences with questions such as "Was I rambling?" or "Did that make any sense?"

- Sisters, don't apologize for needing childcare to serve in ministry. Brothers, don't interrupt, cut off, or ignore a woman while she speaks, or try to mansplain to her what you think she's trying to or ought to say. (If you don't know what mansplaining is, ask a woman to explain it to you.) In meetings, be first to offer to take notes.

7. Don't wait until you feel confident.

- It takes a while to find your voice and feel competent and confident at exercising your God-given gifts. But you have to use your voice in order to find it and exercise your gifts in order to edify others.

- See every opportunity you have to serve as a chance to grow. Setting up chairs, giving announcements, creating or leading liturgies, facilitating a small group, teaching Sunday school, leading worship, praying or reading Scripture publicly, organizing an event—see these opportunities not only as a way to serve others but also as a chance to discern and practice your gifts and grow as a communicator and leader. Invite (as opposed to passively wait for) others to give you constructive, honest feedback for how you can develop and improve.

8. See beyond present, masculine paradigms of leadership.

- I had a T-shirt from seminary that said, "You say I preach like a woman? I say, 'Amen!'" I do preach like a woman because I am a woman, a Korean American woman. Strong and able women leaders are out there, and there is no single image of us that comes to mind. I hope and pray that when my own kids, students, and church members close their eyes and imagine what a capable and Christ-like leader looks like, they imagine women as immediately and vividly as they do men.

- Experiment with team leadership, such as preaching and pastoral teams, that includes women. These team models for leadership make healthier ecclesiology. But forming collaborations requires trial, error, and patience. When we share the weight of leadership between men and women, we serve the body of Christ better because we share out of our strengths, cover our weaknesses, and honor the diversity of Christ's church.

The Vital Responsibility of Making, Sharing, and Holding Space for Others

As Christian leaders, it is our responsibility to foster a more equal pulpit. We need to equip both women and men to interpret the Bible for themselves and their congregations and to forge new partnerships and collaborative configurations that connect the church, the academy, and our larger communities together. Like Mary, we must sit first before we can effectively walk. Even the most seasoned among us need to sit and receive from our Lord before we can rise, empower, and give to others in his name. Our value is not derived from what we do for Jesus. Our value comes from what Jesus has done for us. It's out of this identity as his beloved daughters, sons, disciples, and leaders that we can be empowered, equipped, and encouraged as women to lead and as men to partner with women in *shared* leadership in our churches to the glory of God.

Establishing a more equal pulpit requires that we expand our imaginations for what a preacher looks and sounds like. Our churches need more women in the pulpit proclaiming God's word. We need more women at the table where decisions are being made. And we need more women discipling, training, shepherding, and leading our members. A more equal pulpit must be (en)gendered. By this I mean it has to be brought about by concerted effort, with conviction that it is vital, and with long-term commitment. Women need to receive training and mentoring to mature as church leaders *and* preachers. Women also need frequent opportunities to preach. This is not only for the sake of their vocational discernment and gift development but for the well-being and overall thriving of our churches and ministries.

Mary takes up space at Jesus' feet without apologizing for doing so, even when being misunderstood or judged for her assertive posture. And what is perhaps more surprising is that Jesus makes no apologies for Mary but rather he affirms her, even when being asked to do something about her. In order to have more equal pulpits in our churches, we who are in positions to give women opportunities to preach and help them develop and exercise their voices must be willing to take heat and criticism for doing so without throwing these sister-preachers under the bus.

Just as the other disciples had to be taught by Jesus to accept Mary's presence at what they saw as their table, so congregations need to be discipled into hearing the Word of God proclaimed by women, and discipled out of their thinking only men can speak for God. As Lisa Thompson explains, women who proclaim, women of color, and especially Black women "have to sit with the reminder that people do not readily believe our voices belong at the table; our status is often that of forced outsider."[6] The tension of preaching both as a "forced outsider" and also as one invited to the table by God can creates openings while generatively disrupting negative expectations and long-held beliefs about women in pastoral leadership.[7] Such holy disruptions are not always gentle, and such openings may not give way without resistance. Yet when they are received as the "good portion," they have the potential to help our congregations reimagine what the kingdom of God and what our life together for the sake of the world will look and sound like.

Implications for Today's Pulpit

1. Who are some of the key mentors in your life that have encouraged or inspired you to pursue ministry or church leadership? How can you

---

6. Thompson, *Ingenuity*, 4.
7. Thompson, *Ingenuity*, 4.

be more generous and flexible with the idea of a mentor? How can you be more open to finding mentors in unexpected places?

2. How have you avoided pulling up a seat and taking a place at the table of leadership? In what ways might you need to take up more space at the table and in the pulpit? In what ways can you make space for other women to do so?

3. Do you find it difficult to say no to others without apologizing or feeling guilty? Why do you think this is the case? Why is it okay and even vital and faithful to say no sometimes to demands and requests to serve?

4. What are your current opportunities to serve in ministry? How can you see these opportunities as both a way to serve others and a chance to discern and practice your gifts and to grow as a communicator and leader?

5. Do you find it harder to stand or to sit—to give of yourself or to receive from others? List some practices that can help you take up a posture of receiving and learning. List some practices that can help you offer more generous hospitality and make space of other voices and ways of leading.

6. What possible openings and holy disruptions do you see in your current ministry contexts for engendering a more equal pulpit?

BIBLIOGRAPHY

Gench, Frances Taylor. *Back to the Well: Women's Encounters with Jesus in the Gospels.* Louisville: Westminster John Knox, 2004.

González, Justo L. *Luke.* Belief. Louisville: Westminster John Knox, 2010.

Green, Joel B. *The Gospel of Luke.* New International Commentary on the New Testament. Grand Rapids: Eerdmans, 1997.

Morse, MaryKate. *Making Room for Leadership: Power, Space, and Influence.* Downers Grove, IL: InterVarsity, 2008.

Thompson, Lisa L. *Ingenuity: Preaching as an Outsider.* Nashville: Abingdon, 2018.

6

Mordecai and Esther
Intercultural Negotiation of Power Dynamics

Young Lee Hertig

INTRODUCTION

I ARRIVED IN THE United States in 1981, in St. Paul, Minnesota, where I first began my Korean American second-generation ministry. It started while attending Bethel Theological Seminary, where I chose to study in order to address two issues: the overall lack of public theology and the patriarchal nature of Korean Christianity. On the first issue, I had long struggled with Christianity's lack of public theology. The one exception I found was *minjung* theology among Korean scholars, but even this remained largely irrelevant to the Korean Christian community at large. Regarding the second issue of Korean Christianity's patriarchal nature, I questioned the predominance of male-occupied pulpits which persisted despite the numerical majority status of women in the church. This problem of gender inequality and inequity has troubled me since my teen years, when I nearly abandoned patriarchal Christianity altogether. Counter to Korean culture, I felt as if I viewed Korean Christian culture from the outside in, with many questions, yet with few resources for answers.

In the decades since, my questions remain largely unanswered. During a 2015 women's retreat hosted by the nonprofit I lead, Innovative Space for Asian American Christianity (ISAAC), an Asian American woman began weeping. She shared that because of her gender she had been blocked from fully exercising her spiritual gifts in the church. She reported younger males put on the fast track for ordination while she despite holding a Master of Divinity (MDiv) degree was left serving snacks in between services. Witnessing this degradation of a woman of color's pastoral leadership triggered my memories of weeping with female MDiv students of color at a local seminary where I taught in the early 1990s. Back then, our campus was filled with the energetic voices of gender-inclusive God language and for women's equality in the church. But since then, gender equality and equity issues have been steadily relegated to the back burner in many denominations as LGBTQ and racial justice activism have taken center stage. I have seen Asian American and Pacific Islander (AAPI) male pastors advocating for LGBTQ issues and Black Lives Matter while neglecting the gender inequality in their own churches. But these issues of social justice are not mutually exclusive. They are not part of a zero-sum game. Cries for justice rise to God in each of these cases.

We cannot simply move on from the problem of gender inequality in the pulpit, not while Christian pulpits continue to be monopolized by men, thus normalizing and propagating the masculinization of Christianity. Although some mainline denominations have made strides in attracting more women to the pulpit, evangelical and independent churches are influenced not by the mainline denominations but by American megachurches and their complementarian leaders. Under predominantly male-centered pulpits, women—again, the majority population in such churches—find ourselves facing the choice of either yielding to masculine authority and power or exiting the church altogether.

This pattern is even more pronounced in contemporary ethnic churches such as Asian American and Latino/a congregations. Ethnic churches are often less prone to hiring women clergy—including women who may have come of age in those churches. Thus, many women of color, both ordained and candidates, wind up serving in predominantly Eurpean American churches, the only places where they are afforded the opportunity. Unless pulpits in ethnic churches become more equitable, these churches, defined by their patriarchal culture, will continue to marginalize the voices of the majority in the churches (women), will continue to alienate women leaders and potential leaders who choose not to accommodate to the dominant male leadership culture, and will likely continue to lose women congregants. Pursuing a more equitable pulpit, then, requires unmasking this internalized evangelical narrative shaped by patriarchal epistemology. Although politics are ubiquitous and notorious, rarely do we learn how to be shrewd as Jesus taught his disciples before commissioning them to the mission. Yet, many evangelical women in general either remain naive about shrewdness or engage in futile power mongering.

A male-dominant pulpit, with its symbolic and discursive power backed by male authority over women, harms the body of Christ and reinforces male dominance in the life of the church as well as in the family. We have a long way to go in actualizing gender equality and justice in the church. For such transformation of the pulpit, we will need male coconspirators who open up their pulpits and hire female clergy as equal partners in ministry.

This chapter explores how the partnership between two outsiders, Mordecai and Esther, eventually allows both of them to enter the orbit of King Xerxes and to become insiders. Their work changes the fate of their people, who had teetered on the edge of imminent danger because of the king's vizier Haman, who plotted to eradicate the Jewish people. Mordecai and Esther's navigation of the palace system has ample contemporary implications for navigating contemporary church systems that all too often relegate women to narrow parameters of leadership.

Mordecai and Esther's example serves as a template for the collaboration of men and women in a common mission. As migrants into Xerxes's palace, Mordecai and Esther exhibit spirit-filled cross-cultural power-brokering as they befriend the enemy in order to carry out their mission of saving their people. Thus, they reverse the power of the "other" in order to save their kin. Through multiple twists and turns, Xerxes changes sides and eventually empowers Esther and Mordecai. Ultimately, Xerxes reverses Haman's plot when Haman speaks to the king about hanging Mordecai on the gallows. Haman enters the court, and the king asks him, "What should be done to the man whom the king delights to honor?" (6:6 ESV). Thinking that the king would be honoring Haman himself, Haman suggests that such a person should be paraded through the streets with a royal robe that the King has worn and a horse the King has ridden, one with a royal crest placed on its head. "Go right away," Xerxes commands Haman. "Get the robe. Bring the horse. Do exactly what you have suggested. *Do it for the Jew*

Mordecai" (Esther 6:4–10). Thus, Xerxes, a Gentile king, affirms the Jews' mission in spite of Haman's genocidal plot.

TWO EXTRAORDINARY QUEENS

The book of Esther depicts two extraordinary queens enacting similar and yet unique ploys within the patriarchal palace system. The similarity resides in their "If I perish, I perish" spirit and in their use of banquets to reverse their fortunes. For Queen Vashti, her approach is decidedly more direct. She displays overt courage in her outright refusal to obey King Xerxes's summons to appear at his banquet (seemingly naked), wearing her royal crown (1:10), during the height of their drinking goblets of royal wine. Instead, she hosts a separate palace women's banquet. The magnitude of Vashti's actions speaks loudly, exhibited by the reactions of Xerxes and his officials. Seven lawyers are summoned by the angry king to decide what to do about Vashti's disobedience (1:13–14). They argue that the queen's defiant behaviors will spill over to all other women and endanger the patriarchal system (1:17). To ensure the patriarchy, Xerxes proclaims an edict that "every man should be ruler over his own household" (1:22).

Vashti's overt defiance, bucking the abusive patriarchal system, differs from Esther's covert approach of milking the system to serve her mission. In Esther's case, she executes a series of schemes by tapping into the king's power to thwart an imminent threat of genocide against her people. As a young Jewish girl, Esther/Hadassah conceals her ethnicity through her cousin Mordecai's coaching (3:20) and succeeds Vashti, the deposed queen of Persia. The meanings of her names—Hadassah (righteousness) and Esther (hiddenness)—displays her shrewdness within and her innocence without, in her engagement with the Gentiles in their court. Her attributes preview Christ's instructions to his disciples, "Behold, I am sending you out as sheep in the midst of wolves, so be wise as serpents and innocent as doves" (Matt 10:16).

Since Esther's dual identity requires a both-and lens, I employ a *yinist* epistemology, derived from Taoism, which sees reality through a both-and holism. Yin, the feminine energy in Taoism, includes masculine energy, yang. Likewise, yang, the masculine energy, includes the feminine energy, yin. This concept is paralleled in Jungian psychology where the male's unconscious feminine inner archetype is called *anima* (yin) and the female's counterpart is called *animus* (yang). Based on the idea of yinist wholeness of being and becoming, I examine the two outsiders—Mordecai and Esther—utilizing yin and yang energy for power-brokering within the inner palace. Here, Esther follows Mordecai's coaching and eventually reverses Haman's plot against her people. Mordecai's refusal to pay honor to Haman (3:2) sets an example that parallels Vashti's refusal earlier to honor the king's request.

Mordecai and Esther's work is preceded by Queen Vashti's expulsion from the court. At the time of her removal, Vashti is only sixteen years old. Even more striking, Esther, a Jewish girl, is only fourteen years old. She not only enters the Persian court, but also replaces Vashti as the new queen! So Esther's position in the court is tenuous. She must balance her efforts to influence Xerxes without appearing to be overtly political.

Robert Greene provides historical background on the palace court:

> Throughout history, a court has always formed itself around the person in power—king, queen, emperor, leader. The courtiers who filled this court were in an especially delicate position; they had to serve their masters, but if they seemed to fawn, if they curried favor too obviously, the other courtiers around them would notice and would act against them. Attempts to win the master's favor, then, had to be subtle.[1]

Esther enters the palace, and displaying yin and yang interplay navigates a series of twists and turns that would be at home in a Shakespearian drama. Her mission requires boldness in disguise and the savvy scheme of power-brokering. Her meticulous wielding of power results in the reversing the power dynamics in the banquet hall. It is here in these courtly events where major power-brokering takes place. Therefore banquets feature prominently in the book of Esther, where we find that a total of ten banquets are held:

1. Xerxes's banquet for the nobility (1:2–4)

2. Xerxes's banquet for all the men in Susa (1:5–8)

3. Vashti's banquet for the palace women (1:9)

4. Esther's enthronement banquet (3:15)

5. Haman and Xerxes's banquet (3:15)

6. Esther's first banquet (5: 4–8)

1. Greene, *The 48 Laws of Power*, 1.

7. Esther's second banquet (7:1–9)

8. The Jews' feasting in celebration of Mordecai's glory and the counter-decree (8:17)

9. The first feast of Purim: Ada 14 (9:17, 19)

10. The second feast of Purim: Adar 15 (9:18)[2]

According to Carol M. Bechtel, these banquet scenes set power reversals in motion. For example, the Persian feasts—banquets 1 and 2—contrast with the Purim feasts—banquets 9 and 10. The banquet that causes Vashti's demotion as queen (3) contrasts with Esther's enthronement banquet (4).[3]

This chapter focuses on Esther's banquets (6 and 7). These two events display Esther's mission, as she courageously and tactfully maneuvers King Xerxes and the highest officials on her banquet VIP list. In Esther's banquets, four main actors play out their assigned roles—Esther, King Xerxes, Mordecai, and Haman—each experiencing reversals of power. Mixing inner shrewdness and outer innocence, Esther embodies the meanings of her two names—the righteousness of Hadassah and the hiddenness of Esther. In doing so, Esther is equipped to deal with the king and his palace people, embodying Robert Greene's supposition that "the better you are at dealing with power, the better friend, lover, husband, wife, and person you become."[4]

In this delicate pulling of the levers of power, Esther is taking five major risks: (1) the risk of concealing Jewish ethnicity, (2) the risk of becoming queen and having to conceal her identity, (3) the risk of calling every Jew to a three-day fast (the first Purim), (4) the risk of appearing at the king's court without a summons from him, (5) and the risk of hosting a series of banquets. All five risks taken by Esther, as well as those risks taken by Mordecai, involve meticulous decision-making by the Jews in the Persian court.

1. Concealed Jewish Ethnicity

There is a politically savvy saying from seasoned leaders: "Don't volunteer unnecessary information." In order to hide her Jewishness, Hadassah

---

2. See the insightful analysis of the ten banquets in the book of Esther in Bechtel, *Esther*, 5–6.

3. Bechtel, *Esther*, 5.

4. Greene, *The 48 Laws of Power*, 6.

(righteousness) enters the Persian palace with a Persian name, Esther (hiddenness). She conceals her nationality and family background per Mordecai's advice (2:10).

2. Becoming Queen

Esther comes upon the scene as an orphan raised by her cousin, Mordecai. Together they enter into the enemy's palace in order to succeed Queen Vashti. It is Esther's extraordinary beauty that grants her entry into King Xerxes's palace. Esther then receives an elaborate twelve months of beauty treatment (2:12) before succeeding Vashti (2:17), who had relinquished her position as a result of her revolt against patriarchal demands. Robert Greene, in *The 48 Laws of Power*, offers a countercultural approach to dealing with enemies that parallels Mordecai and Esther's approach to the Persian palace:

> Be wary of friends—they will betray you more quickly, for they are easily aroused to envy. They also become spoiled and tyrannical. But hire a former enemy and he will be more loyal than a friend, because he has more to prove. In fact, you have more to fear from friends than from enemies. If you have no enemies, find a way to make them.[5]

Usually we disengage from our enemies. We do not usually treat them as friends, let alone marry them. Yet it is by engaging them at the right time that mutual benefits emerge. Rival parties can come together for a purpose as long as we can manage, as Napoleon Bonaparte famously stated, to "place our iron hand inside a velvet glove." Further, Greene instructs, "Power requires the ability to play with appearances: to this end you must learn to wear many masks and keep a bag full of deceptive tricks."[6] This statement is prone to being misunderstood and thus merits explanation. Do the ends (does the mission) justify the means? Not necessarily. In Esther's case, she risks boldly, entering the enemy's space with a hidden identity; her actions show the character of her new name, Esther. In working within a powerful system, it is sometimes necessary to conceal one's identity until the right proper time comes.

---

5. Greene, *The 48 Laws of Power*, 1.
6. Greene, *The 48 Laws of Power*, 1.

3. Purim

Esther calls for collective fasting among Jews before she embarks on her mission. This sets the tone of her mission and solidifies her courage, *a courage* that involves not a lack of fear, but action in spite of fear. Even with all her meticulous and savvy plans, Esther needs this foundational sense of purpose to execute her mission. Rollo May, in *Courage to Create*, explains that "a chief characteristic of courage requires a centeredness within our own being . . . Therefore, it is the foundation that underlies and gives reality to all other virtues and personal values. Without courage, our love pales into mere dependency."[7]

For Esther, it is her calling a collective three-day fast that helps her center her inner self and focus on the divine mission for her people. Such an act reveals her courage and commitment. The required mission and the person to execute it match seamlessly. The extraordinary personality that imbues the spiritualty of "If I perish, I perish" (Esth 4:16) makes the impossible possible. Whereas many cross-cultural mission endeavors are botched by a mismatch between mission and personnel, Esther's qualities, despite her young age, demonstrate the maturity of a sage, raised and coached by her cousin, Mordecai. It is when she calls for collective fasting that she becomes a queen with a mission beyond wearing a gown and royal crown. It is no wonder that adherents of Judaism today celebrate Purim to remember how the Jews spared because of Esther's courage. Contemporary people, with our short attention spans and scattered interests, surely need a spiritual anchoring of the kind that the first Purim gave Esther. All her actions flow out of her courage based on the spirituality of Purim and her motto of "If I perish, I perish." When one does not cling to life, one is free to execute the mission despite the risks involved (cf. Luke 17:33).

4. Approaching the King without a Summons

Esther's bold action of approaching King Xerxes without a summons effectively reversed the King's summoning power, a power with the authority to end her life. The very act of appearing before her husband (in effect summoning him) is an act of defiance that could have gotten Esther killed. Instead, Esther prompts King Xerxes to bend his own rules, and he welcomes her. The unlikely reversal of power between the king and queen is indeed

---

7. May, *The Courage to Create*, 3.

notable, as this "outside-in" mission transforms both the Jewish people and the Persian court power dynamics.

5. Hosting a Series of Banquets

The story of the ousted Queen Vashti must have spread far and wide in the Persian Empire, and Queen Esther, as Vashti's successor, would have heard about the infamous and subversive palace women's banquet that deposed Vashti from her queenship. Esther's bold and meticulous contextual actions—hosting a series of her own banquets—earns her enough favor with the king to foil a genocide plotted by Haman, the king's top official, and to bring death to Haman himself.

Through these five extraordinary acts of courage and faith, Esther indeed places her iron hand inside a velvet glove and outmaneuvers her opponents. In fact, she masters the art of outmaneuvering. Furthermore, Mordecai sets the example for her of being savvy in exile, as he walks "back and forth in front of the court of the harem to find out about Esther's well-being and what was happening to her" (2:11). Mordecai likely served as one of the porters at the main entrance to the palace. In that capacity, he manages to gain information about Esther's progress on the mission of delivering her people. This reveals his shrewdness amid persecution and in defense of the very existence of the Jews and he passes on his shrewd to his adopted daughter, Esther.

In both seminaries and churches, power-brokering is a silent but salient issue. According to *Merriam-Webster.com*, a power broker refers to "a person (as in politics) able to exert strong influence through control of votes or individuals."[8] Institutions are loaded with unhealthy power exigencies. Often the old boy network prevents women from leadership or decision-making. According to Willie James Jennings, "Patriarchy produces a counterfeit vision of God that easily aligns itself with a Christian doctrine of God, kills it, and then replaces it with itself."[9]

In attempts to overcome the patriarchy that dominates the pulpit today, we can follow the examples of both Vashti and Esther. Vashti shows us how to stand in overt defiance against injustice, a powerful lesson with lasting applications. While faith leaders who are women of color continue

8. *Merriam-Webster.com* (website) s.v., "power broker" (https://www.merriam-webster.com/dictionary/power%20broker).

9. Jennings, "A Christian Vision of Belonging," 32.

to be rebuffed and barred from the very pulpits we seek equity in, we also learn from Esther's approach to be savvy in navigating patriarchal pulpits alongside insiders—male pastors and church leaders.

CONTEMPORARY APPLICATION

Since choosing to leave an endowed chair in a theological palace in 2002, I've come to see myself as a theological and missional broker, and thus I resonate deeply with both Vashti and Esther. Like Vashti, I bucked the system when it sapped my life-giving energy. I find Vashti's choice to be in solidarity with the palace women, the king's objects for his own pleasure and design, life-giving and life-risking. No doubt it is an act of self-interest, not self-sacrifice, to choose to be in solidarity with the palace women for their human dignity, even if only momentarily. Jesus' paradoxical truth sheds light: "For whoever would save his life will lose it, but whoever loses his life for my sake and the gospel's will save it" (Mark 8:35). There are times in life when one is called to make courageous and risky decisions simply to keep souls intact. Vashti's disobedience to the king's demand and her exemplary action of organizing a women's banquet as an alternative to the king's, are authentic and powerful initiatives that lead to an unintended consequence—a major threat to the patriarchy, which leaves King Xerxes in a state of powerlessness, desperately consulting his experts for answers.

Meanwhile, in Queen Esther, I find a gentle savviness that utilizes the system to execute her mission. In Esther's story, I see *ethnicity*, *gender*, and *generation* (what together in an acronym I call EGG) working in seamless synchronicity. Esther's story does not feature the usual conflict that these elements often provoke. Ethnically, it is noble for King Xerxes, a Persian, to act counterculturally when he chooses solidarity with the Jewish queen's ethnicity. Genderwise (that is, as a woman) it is noble for Esther to navigate the mission of saving her people by soliciting the king's favor and arranging alternative plans right under his nose. Generationally, it is noble to see a father figure, Mordecai, working together seamlessly with Esther through mutual respect and reciprocity in carrying out the mission of saving the Jews from genocide. These examples are much needed today when the abuse of power is on raw display and threatens law and order, democracy, and integrity; in our time when ethnicity, gender, and generation are often discrediting factors in public policies and procedures.

The example of Esther's relationship with Mordecai underscores the importance of women seeking, in addition to women mentors, male mentors like Mordecai to deal with patriarchal power structures. Across gender and generation, Mordecai and Esther together meticulously execute their bold and risky mission of "If I perish, I perish." Blending the strengths and weaknesses resulting from their differences in gender and generation, both Mordecai and Esther show what it takes to work as power brokers in Xerxes's palace while wielding iron fists in velvet gloves. The stories of Esther and Mordecai serve as an intergenerational and gender bridge today, which is rare but much needed, for a mission that extends beyond individual generations. Language barriers in immigrant communities disconnect generations, which causes a scarcity of intergenerational bridges. Collaboration between male and female leaders in the faith communities also pose challenges due to the dominance of complementarian rather than egalitarian gender roles. Mordecai and Esther provide a contrast through their egalitarian collaboration.

Together, both male and female faith leaders must work compassionately and meticulously in a world plagued by inequalities and exclusionary systems of power. Daring to say, no to abusive power, and to organize people on the margins, confronts the systems in place. Once we wean off of our addictions to self-interest and self-promotion, transformation becomes truly of the people, by the people, and for the people. We thus restore the image of God for both males and females, for insiders and outsiders—all for God's greater mission. Indeed, throughout the Bible, God utilizes many outsiders to teach insiders. The celebration of Purim even today retells the stories of God's provisions for Jews in exile through their entrance into the Persian palace. The implications of diaspora in the book of Esther speak to issues of violence and tension that intensify and deepen today. In this story, Jews in exile transform the Persian king and impact his decision-making. In this dynamic encounter of Jews and Gentiles, both need paradigm shifts as they engage one another: much as King Xerxes bends his policy for Esther after Esther engages him in the palace at risk of her very life. Each transforms and is transformed by the other.

IMPLICATIONS FOR TODAY'S PULPIT

1. In what ways do you observe gender oppression in the church when women of color seek their ordination path?

2. How have you supported and advocated for women faith leaders to pursue ordination as Mordecai supported and advocated for Esther? How can you continue to do so in light of Mordecai's example?

3. How have you navigated and negotiated systemic obstacles in your life? How would you translate your experiences of obstacles toward more an equal pulpit?

BIBLIOGRAPHY

Bechtel, Carol M. *Esther*. Interpretation: A Bible Commentary for Teaching and Preaching. Louisville: Westminster John Knox, 2011.
Greene, Robert. *The 48 Laws of Power*. New York: Penguin, 2000.
May, Rollo. *The Courage to Create*. New York: Norton, 1975.
Jennings, Willie James. "A Christian Vision of Belonging: Gender Identity in the Church." *Society of Asian North American Christian Studies Journal* (2015) 30–40.

7

A Call from an API Male Cooconspirator

NEAL D. PRESA

Some of the Pharisees in the crowd said to him, "Teacher, order your disciples to stop." He answered, "I tell you, if these were silent, the stones would shout out."

—LUKE 19:39–40

ALLOW ME TO SPEAK directly to those who believe, in the core of their being, that God has limited leadership in the church to men, and with that the authority, legitimacy, and ability to proclaim and teach the oracles of the Lord. I wish to speak to that part of the conservative evangelical's heart that views a complementarian reading of the Scripture as the only authoritative and efficacious reading of the Bible. I desire to lean into that mindset that is dead set against any notion of women serving in the ordered ministries of the church—a mindset proffered for centuries in a number of ecclesiastical traditions, grounded upon the Scriptures of the Old and New Testaments. In this chapter, I will speak to the two texts in the New Testament that have been used to limit women from the ordered ministries of the church, the contexts of those texts, and my personal subtext as a male, Filipino American, pastoral ecumenical liturgical theologian.

In this chapter, I will speak along the following lines:

- A brief autobiography as it relates to this question
- The two predominant texts characteristically used to limit women from the ordered ministries of the church: 1 Cor 14:33–36 and 1 Tim 2:11–14
- The authority of Scripture

The conclusion will be the following:

- A faithful reading of 1 Cor 14:33–36 and 1 Tim 2:11–14 is one that seeks proper and orderly worship with apostolic doctrine, love for the community, as the whole people of God bears witness to God's saving work in Jesus Christ through the Holy Spirit.

- The authority of Scripture is not broached or contravened but in fact is affirmed by an egalitarian hermeneutic that highlights the role of God in Christ through the Spirit as all humanity is equalized in Christ and the wholeness of who we are as human beings is lifted up in Christ.

- A faithful reading, interpretation, and application of 1 Cor 14:33–36 and 1 Tim 2:11–14 that dignifies women as equally apostolic, prophetic preachers and teachers as men will express the fullness of the church's unity, holiness, catholicity, and apostolicity.

A BRIEF AUTOBIOGRAPHY

I was born into a Filipino American family in which I was baptized in the Roman Catholic Church through my father's side, and raised in the tradition of the United Church of Christ in the Philippines through my mother's side. This meant that until I came to faith as a teenager, Sunday mornings were split between attending the Catholic church and our Filipino American congregation. Coming to faith as a teenager brought me to delving deeply into study of Scripture and into theology, specifically Reformed theology. While I thought I was headed to law school, God directed my heart instead to theological education, to ministry, and to Westminster Seminary California, where I was exposed to the conservative branch of the Reformed theological tradition. Little did I know when I joined the Presbyterian Church (U.S.A.) in the late 1990s, that my education and engagement in the breadth of the Reformed tradition would set me on a lifelong journey of ministry for the church ecumenical.

While I focused my education at Westminster on theology and history courses, it was clear that the seminary's commitments were decidedly for men in the ordered ministries of the church. I could not square that doctrinal and theological commitment with God's wide covenantal promises for Jews and Gentiles, the prophetic words of Joel 2:28–32 (repeated again at Pentecost in Acts 2:17–21) of the Lord prophesying through women and men, and the first witnesses of Christ's rising on Easter morning being some of Jesus's female followers. I could not see how that branch of the Reformed theological tradition could set aside the apostle Paul's affirmation and commendation of women colaborers in the ministry. These biblical and theological fault lines came to my mind and heart at a time when my beloved maternal grandmother, who raised me in the Christian faith, who was a Bible teacher in our congregation, and who was a charter member of our congregation, was battling an aneurysm, which turned into five years of hospitalization and convalescence.

In ecclesial and ecclesiastical practice, in scriptural interpretation, and in embracing and internalizing the basic humanity of who we are, the Lord helped me to see that women have been leading, are leading, and ought to lead in every aspect of the church and in society. This means that to be faithful to God, to be faithful to Scripture, and to be faithful witnesses of the gospel, the church must permit women to be leaders—preachers and teachers and eucharistic presiders. To not permit women to lead, to restrict or limit women in church leadership, is to deny their humanity, to stifle the work and call of the Holy Spirit, to diminish the church's witness of Christ's full reconciliation of all of humanity, and to subjugate the teachings of Scripture to certain human ways of thinking and acting.

Beginning with my ordination to the ministry of Word and Sacrament in the Presbyterian Church (U.S.A.) in 2003, I set out to advocate and support women in every way, particularly women of color. I continued this work into my PhD studies in 2004, and then as I became active in the modern ecumenical movement in 2006. The gospel's witness of reconciliation, freedom, and what it means to be whole in our humanity is diminished by not supporting and empowering women. This means, at minimum, faithfulness to the gospel entails supporting women in their sense of calling to serve in every area of church leadership. Living the gospel faithfully and fully also means critiquing theologies and ideologies that limit women, reforming systems and institutions so that women, especially women of color, are recognized for who they are; so that they are supported in their vocational callings; so that any violence against women in words, deeds, or attitudes is challenged; and so that perpetrators of violence against women are brought to transformative justice.

By the time I became Moderator of the 220th General Assembly of the Presbyterian Church (U.S.A.) (serving from 2012 to 2014), our governing council's highest elected national official, I had a track record of commitments to ecumenism, advocacy for racial and gender justice, and appointing people of color (with an emphasis on women of color) to the national church entities. At every opportunity for exercising moderatorial prerogatives on national committees, task forces, and working groups, I made sure that a majority of those appointments were to people of color, with a special emphasis on women of color. While every General Assembly Moderator appoints at least five of the sixteen members of the General Assembly Nominating Committee, four of my appointments were women of color and two were men of color. By making these appointments, I intentionally and strategically tilted the General Assembly Nominating Committee for the subsequent two years to have a majority of persons of color.

COMMON TEXTS: 1 CORINTHIANS 14:33-36 AND 1 TIMOTHY 2:11-14

The literature commending both complementarian and egalitarian views of the role of women in church leadership and the ordination of women are plentiful. Simply google or go to an online library catalog and you will find shelves of books on this subject along with official church statements and pronouncements from mainline and conservative churches adhering to one or the other of these perspectives. Those don't need repeating here. I can present an exhaustive exegesis of the two main texts cited to limit women in church leadership—1 Cor 14:33-36 and 1 Tim 2:11-14. I can cite this commentary or that biblical expert, but that alone won't convince you. As I briefly charted in my ecclesial journey, let me share how the Lord led me to understand how those texts squared with their biblical contexts and with the overall thrust of God's work in covenant history as witnessed to in Scripture.

I began my study of Scripture in my teenage years, developing into a more astute student in seminary and then as a pastor and as a theologian.

My academic field beyond my theological educational training is in liturgical and ecumenical theology. This means I care deeply for and know much about the histories and theologies of Christian worship and the sustained work of the church in seeking visible unity in the midst of our theological and ecclesiastical differences. These elements permeate liturgical scholarship. Paul F. Bradshaw, the renowned scholar of early church history and liturgy, posited that there were diverse expressions of Christian worship in the first four centuries of the early church, and that many house churches followed the patterns of synagogue worship so that the leadership of these churches was quite possibly held by women together with men:[1] this would square with the apostle Paul's commendation of women as ministry co-laborers. Gary Macy has also written an extensive volume on women in ordained ministries in the medieval West.[2]

Yet in the contemporary church, ordered ministries are too often restricted only to men, and 1 Cor 14:33–36 and 1 Tim 2:11–14 are cited as the two go-to passages to justify this limiting. The usual argument is that while God honors and has gifted all people, God has called only men to exercise spiritual and governance leadership in the life of the church. Such patterning is said to follow the patriarchs of the Old Testament, and Jesus's calling of men as the twelve disciples. Further, while women are gifted to teach, being faithful means being obedient to the injunction of Scripture to direct those gifts to what the Scriptures permit. This so-called regulative principle states that one can only do what the Scriptures explicitly warrant, and that one cannot do what the Scriptures explicitly prohibit.

The problem with this approach to these two texts, or to any scriptural texts for that matter, lies in the exegetical gymnastics that one must perform in order to comport with our lived experience. The Corinthian text says that "women should be silent," that "they are not permitted to speak," and that if women seek to know a matter "let them ask their husbands at home" because "it is shameful for a woman to speak in church." Several problems persist:

- Does God seek total, complete silence from women in the church? My erstwhile teachers tried to explain this text by saying that women can speak in church provided that they teach other women or young people, so long as they are not in positions of authority over men. I

---

1. See Bradshaw et al., *The Apostolic Tradition*.
2. See Macy, *The Hidden History*.

asked in one setting, Well, what would happen if a woman was teaching a Bible study for women and then a man walked in? Would she have to stop teaching?

- Can women ask only their husbands if they want to know something in the church? Such a prescription assumes that a woman is married. If she's not married, to whom can she turn? Surely conservative evangelicals who herald the model of the two-parent household will not allow a single woman to consult someone else's husband for guidance! My maternal grandmother, who endured a rough divorce in the Philippines, who raised six children and twelve grandchildren, and who was a faithful teacher and leader in our Filipino American church, did not have a husband for decades. Was she sinning by seeking out the guidance of other men and women in the church because she didn't have a husband to ask guidance from?

- When God's people have a testimony to share, when God's people have a praise to sing, does God silence them? Such a proscription to completely silence women would contradict the Psalms' clear exhortation for all of God's creation to praise the Lord: "Let everything that breathes praise the Lord!" (Ps 150:6)

The context of the Corinthian text shows us what is happening. First Corinthians 14:33–36 appears within a letter concerned about orderliness in the church's worship because of ongoing disorder caused by theological divisions becoming partisan (chapter 3); sexual immorality (chapter 5); litigation between church members (chapter 6); caring for those who were single or widowed (chapter 7); offering food to idols, eating such food, or both; (chapter 8); abusing the sacredness of the Lord's Table (chapters 10 and 11); and exercising spiritual gifts in ways that may cause division (chapter 12 and chapter 14)—particularly in praying, speaking in tongues, interpreting the tongues, or playing music (14:26). Just as the criteria in 1 Cor 13 that all things done in the church be done out of love, so all exercise of gifts are to be "done for building up" (13:26). What is in view in 1 Cor 14:33–36 is not women speaking per se, but particular women in the Corinthian church, who, like others in the Corinthian church, are causing disorder in the church by speaking, teaching, prophesying, interpreting, serving, or singing in ways that are not building up the whole body; they are not acting within the church out of love. The closing verses of chapter 14 say this: "and do not forbid speaking in tongues; but all things should be done decently and in order" (vv. 39b–40). Both women and men spoke and speak tongues. The clear admonition is not to forbid the speaking in tongues, but to remind that speaking in tongues requires a clear and orderly interpretation, and that the exercise of that gift equips and strengthens the whole body and does not inure to the speaker the glory of speaking, or somehow diminish the glory and praise of God within the speaker. Thus, the thrust of Corinthians in both the whole and its parts is an orderliness of the church's worship life and fellowship that attends to the teaching of apostolic doctrine, that honors the whole as well as every individual member of the community, and that those who teach and exercise a public gift are to do so with the aim of supporting the equipping the whole body of Christ. It is not a proscription for women specifically, as if women are to be ashamed, or that their speaking is shameful; rather what is to be addressed in this particular instance, in Corinth and in other churches connected to the apostle Paul, are the men and women alike who speak and prophesy even though the whole body is not being equipped; Paul's specific address-ees here are women and men whose teaching and prophesying are not done in love for the whole body.

The Corinthian text moves to chapter 15, which centers on the gospel of Jesus Christ. After addressing the specific contextual challenges of the Corinthian church in the midst of Gentile idolatry and the proliferation of heresy, the apostle Paul sees resolution in the power and promise of the good news of God in Christ: "Now I would remind you, brothers and sisters, of the good news that I proclaimed to you, which you in turn received, in which also you stand, through which also you are being saved, if you hold firmly to the message that I proclaimed to you" (15:1–2). He proceeds to share the gospel—the life, death, and resurrection of Jesus Christ—and by doing so both prescribes and proscribes what the Corinthians are to do. The prescription is that they (and we!) are to "come to a sober and right mind, and sin no more . . . be steadfast, immovable, always excelling in the work of the Lord" (15:34; 16:58). The proscription is to avoid questioning whether the resurrection is an accomplished fact: "how can some of you say there is no resurrection from the dead?" We can infer that the reality of Christ's resurrection was in question, and presumably some prophets and teachers were encouraging this questioning in the Corinthian church. For Paul, the certainty of Christ's resurrection isn't just about apostolic doctrine and the correct transmission of the tradition of the life, death, and resurrection; it is also about what the reality of the risen life of Jesus Christ is doing in the life of the ecclesial community. Is the focus of people's action about themselves, or is it about the upbuilding of the love of the community—to love God and to love neighbor? Insofar as litigation among believers, the eating of food sacrificed to idols, sexual immorality, and disorderly conduct in teaching, preaching, and prophesying obscure the love of God in Christ, then such actions are to stop. What is not in view is an outright prohibition of half of the Corinthian church membership (the women) to cease all speech; to cease all proclamation; to cease all testimony and witness of the resurrection; to be silent in praising and proclaiming the truth of Christ's life, death, and resurrection to children, women, and men in the church community and in the external community. To issue such a prohibition to all women would be to subvert the freedom of the resurrection in freeing God's people to bear witness of God's love in Jesus Christ in the power of the Holy Spirit.

First Timothy 2:11–14 has similar textual and contextual dynamics to 1 Cor 14:33–36. Timothy, an apostolic protégé of Paul, is being exhorted here to attend to the ecclesial life of churches as an outward witness of the gospel. One of the marks of faithful living in community is prayer and supplication "for everyone, for kings and all who are in high positions, so that we may lead a quiet and peaceable life in all godliness and dignity" (1 Tim 2:1–2). Life, both individual and communal, is to be marked by love, by gratitude, by moderation and humility that builds up the whole body and does not draw attention to oneself. In line with concerns generally expressed in the New Testament, here Paul amplifies the importance of pursuing conduct befitting of the gospel, and of living lives that are shaped by the apostolic doctrine. The letter says as much in the opening verses:

> I urge you, as I did when I was on my way to Macedonia, to remain in Ephesus so that you may instruct certain people not to teach any different doctrine, and not to occupy themselves with myths and endless genealogies that promote speculations rather than divine training that is known by faith. But the aim of such instruction is love that comes from a pure heart, a good conscience, and sincere faith. Some people have deviated from these and turned to meaningless talk, desiring to be teachers of the law, without understanding either what they are saying or the things about which they make assertions. (1:3–7)

Right thinking and right living go hand in hand. The New Testament and the first four centuries of the Christian churches were focused on insuring the transmission, preservation, and contextual application of apostolic teachings for the advancement of Christ's teachings after his ascension. There was a related concern as to how the promises of the covenant related to both Jews and Gentiles, and what the gospel's witness looked like in the daily lives of new converts as well as in the ecclesial life of nascent churches. Related to both belief and practice was the charism of humility, and with that, gratitude for who God is and who we are in God—thus, the distinction of Creator and creatures, divine and human.

The thrust of 1 Tim 2 is in its accent on the divine-human distinction, not on gender distinctions. The chapter begins with the pastoral exhortation to pray for everyone no matter how high or low someone is in the socioeconomic and political structures of the day (vv. 1–3). Why? The reason given is that God "desires everyone to be saved and to come to the knowledge of the truth" (v. 4). The text continues: Because of the truth of Jesus Christ, the apostle Paul has been appointed a teacher and an apostle. Because of this calling, Paul desires for men to pray peaceably, and for women to wear modest clothes and not to teach or have authority, because Adam was not deceived but Eve was (vv. 5–13). What is Paul addressing when his excursus takes a sudden turn from speaking about the general practice of praying for everyone to the universality of God's mediatorship in Christ (vv. 5–6) to the specification of Paul's apostolic calling (v. 7)? Why does he then direct his attention to exhorting men to pray "without anger or argument" (v. 8) when the universal calling to pray has already been given in v. 1? And why does he then address the attire of women (vv. 9–10), from which he then proscribes women from speaking and having authority (vv. 11–12)? And to drive the nail in the coffin, so to speak, on any possibility of women speaking or having authority, the argument goes that the apostle Paul cites the order of creation (Eve came from Adam; Eve caused Adam to sin) to universalize the application on the basis of the ontology of woman and man (vv. 13–14). But is that what is going on in this passage?

The traditional, complementarian interpretation of this passage is problematic on several fronts. All people—men and women alike—are to pray; that is the exhortation in 1 Tim 2:1, as it is in 1 Thess 5:17 ("Pray without ceasing"). So to specify that men should pray and that they should pray in this way is to specify that certain men in the churches Timothy is serving are not doing that—that they are presumably praying with anger or with an argumentative attitude, or not praying as often as would befit their calling as ones redeemed in Christ; for the posture of prayer anchors men and women alike to the God, "who desires everyone to be saved and to come to the knowledge of the truth" (2:4). The prescription is not exclusive to men; it applies to women; it applies to children. The apostle Paul is advising Timothy on this score because of specific incidents of disorder, or a laxity on the part of some men in the churches, who are not praying consistently, or who are praying in a way that is not peaceable. Likewise, the next exhortation for women's modest attire and coiffure (vv. 9–10) is addressing specific incidents of ostentation encountered by Timothy in the churches. Why? The call for modesty and humility in all things is attendant on all people. It is not just women. Men and children are also to be modest and humble; otherwise ostentation and pomp will direct attention to the ostentatious person, to their financial resources that give them the ability to purchase the jewelry, or the hairdos and Easter hats that would block one's view of the pulpit and the preacher. In other words, Paul is again addressing specific incidents that Timothy encounters where some women in the churches are not wearing modest attire or coiffure, drawing attention to themselves.

Finally, we confront the exhortation for women to learn in submission and in silence because of the creational order of Eve coming after Adam, and of Eve as the one deceived and the transgressor. It is helpful for my students to listen to their professor and even for my teenage sons to listen to their father when I am speaking. They likewise appreciate it when I listen when they are speaking and teaching me something. We all are teachers and we all are students, to varying degrees and levels. And the relational dynamics of teaching and learning are made decent and orderly (in learning) when there is a desire and posture to receive what is being taught and to engage the subject matter and the one doing the instruction. Here again, in 1 Timothy the apostle Paul is addressing a specific pastoral concern in the churches that presumably involves some unnamed women causing disorder, usurping authority, not teaching apostolic doctrine, and/ or not respecting the apostolic leadership in those churches. Again, such an exhortation is applicable to everyone: women, men, and children alike. We desire and expect every member of the community to respect authority, to learn and teach peaceably; that showing consistent disregard and disrespect for the community and causing disorder in both manner and teaching would call for the disruptive individual or individuals to cease and desist.

As to the reason for the pastoral exhortation, the traditional, complementarian interpretation anchors the directive for silence and authority on the supposed ontological priority of Adam over Eve in terms of the sequence of creation, the derivative nature of Eve with respect to Adam, and the apostle's description of Eve as the one who was deceived and was the transgressor. Such a reading of the text views the order of creation as rational rather than as an analogy. Felix Cortez argues forcefully that the order of creation should be read as an analogy; for example, the apostle Paul reads creation's order as an analogy in 1 Cor 11:11–12 with respect to the specific Corinthian exhortation for women to wear a veil. ("Nevertheless, in the Lord woman is not independent of man or man independent of woman. For just as woman came from man, so man comes through woman; but all things come from God" [1 Cor 14:11–12]).[3] First Timothy 2:13–14 reads the creation ordering from the perspective of the fall, which resulted in human sinfulness proliferating—one form of which is gender-based subordination and skewing God's initial egalitarian design before the fall. First Corinthians 11:11–12 highlight the egalitarian ontology restored in Christ whereby man and woman come through each other, are interdependent, and both (as all things do) "come from God." This also squares with the oft-quoted comprehensive result of Christ's salvation: "There is no longer Jew or Greek, there is no longer slave or free, there is no longer male and female; for all of you are one in Christ Jesus" (Gal 3:28). This interpretive framework comports well with Peter's recapitulation of the Old Testament prophecy of Joel in his Pentecost sermon: "In the last days it will be, God declares, that I will pour out my Spirit upon all flesh, and your sons and your daughters shall prophesy, and your young men shall see visions, and our old men shall dream dreams. Even upon my slaves, both men and women, in those days I will pour out my Spirit; and they shall prophesy" (Acts 2:17–18; cf. Joel 2:28–29). Additionally, Cortez reminds us that even importing the modern understanding of the word "helper" to the Near East understanding of "helper" is problematic in that the Near East usage was expressed in contexts such as when kings sought a foreign power to be a "helper" for conquest. Far from opening up an asymmetrical relationship, such a situation involved equals coming together for common cause. In short, these efforts and practices—to subordinate women, to silence women, and to diminish their role as "helpers" to men, relegating them to learn in their homes under the instruction of their husbands—result from misreadings and misapplications of the texts before us on several scores. First, the apostle Paul is addressing specific incidents of disorder in the

3. See Cortez, "The Argument of the Order of Creation in 1 Timothy 2:9–15."

churches in Timothy's charge at and near Ephesus. The exhortation applies to all the believers (women, men, children); the whole body is to attend to the decent and orderly nature of teaching and learning. All community members are equal to one to another and in the sight of God, for all are redeemed in Christ and are to submit equally to his authority, and all are equally responsible to support and encourage one another and the whole body for the witness of the gospel.

THE AUTHORITY OF SCRIPTURE

Proponents of the traditional, complementarian interpretation of 1 Cor 14:33–36 and 1 Tim 2:11–14 warn that interpreting these passages in an egalitarian way and thereby authorizing and legitimizing women in leadership in the church would threaten the authority of Scripture, disregard Scripture's plain teaching, be a willful act of disobedience to God's Word, and so be an intentional sinful act against the holy God who inspired the Scriptures to be written, and who inspired believers, such as the apostle Paul and succeeding apostolic leaders, to follow those divine directives. Furthermore, traditional complementarians point to the notion that the inerrant and infallible character of Scripture is derived from the inerrant and infallible character of the holy God whose word and will accomplish that which the Lord deems it to do (Isa 55:11). Thus, so say traditional complementarians, to not follow the mandates of 1 Cor 14:33–36 and 1 Tim 2:11–14 is to not take Scripture seriously, is to not be a careful student of the Scriptures, is to ignore the Scriptures, is to ignore the God who is the author of those Scriptures, and is to commit a crime against the Lord. Does this line of reasoning sound familiar to you? Do you hold to this belief?

Let's be clear. All believers (I am not making any distinction as to what is meant by *liberal, progressive,* or *conservative*; nor am I speaking of any one theological tradition or ecclesial polity) are enjoined to worship, serve, and love the holy God, and to trust that we are loved by God. We are enjoined to receive, meditate upon, read, reflect upon, be instructed by, and be guided by the Scriptures of the Old and New Testaments (Ps 19), for they are words inspired by God (2 Tim 3:16), and being inspired from God's heart and coming from God's desire for us, the Scriptures are to be received as loving truth from God to us. Secondly, the authority of Scripture is inherent not in what we as human beings attribute to it, but in its very nature as coming from the heart of God for us. This means that what we do or don't do does not diminish or augment the inherent authority of Scripture. The Scriptures are the Scriptures, just as God is God. Someone who does not acknowledge God's existence does not diminish at all God's existence and God's reality; God is God, the I AM is the I AM. So, whether we devote ten hours to studying Scripture or ten years to studying Scripture, our efforts or lack thereof, our comprehension or lack thereof, our efforts to interpret or lack thereof, do not in any way contribute to the inherent authority of Scripture.

Additionally, the Scriptures are to be wrestled with in the community of believers. Even before the oral tradition took on written form, God's speech-acts to the patriarchs and matriarchs of the faith were received and wrestled with in communities of judges, prophets, teachers, rabbis, disciples, and apostles who argued among themselves, and who applied the Scriptures to their individual lives and in their communities as best as they could with the prime directive of the two greatest commandments: love God with all of your heart, with all of your soul, with all of your mind, and with all of your strength; and love your neighbor as yourself (Matt 22:37–40; Mark 12:29–31; cf. Luke 10:25–28). Holding on to the authority of Scripture, therefore, is understood to be how the body of believers wrestles and grapples with the Scriptures, prays for the guidance and leading of the Holy Spirit, and seeks the wise counsel and teaching of other teachers (theologians). The authority of Scripture is recognized by the community's and an individual's desire to search for God's leading and direction so that the process and the outcome, the intent and the impact, are towards loving God and loving neighbor more deeply, more widely, and more truly.

When it comes then to 1 Cor 14:33–36 and 1 Tim 2:11–14 and recognizing, authorizing, supporting, legitimizing, blessing, and supporting women in the ordered ministries of the church, particularly in senior pastoral leadership, this is not a question about the authority of Scripture as has been understood with the traditional issues of inerrancy, infallibility, and obedience to the plain reading of the scriptural text. The question has more to do with how believers in every age, and certainly how we as twenty-first-century Christians, grapple with passages such as these two in light of the core and thrust of the biblical narrative in the Old and New Testaments, in light of the core and thrust of the gospel, and in light of what it means for our divine-human and human-human relationships and engagement.

Egalitarian readings, interpretations, and applications of 1 Cor 14:33–36 and 1 Tim 2:11–14 are in sync with God's intentions for all of creation, directly correlate with the mission and character of the gospel, and reorient the divine-human and human-human relationships and engagement towards love and to the God who is love. God created all human beings in the image of God, and, therefore, equal in the sight of the Lord—equal in our brokenness, equally in need of God's mercy, and equally redeemed in Jesus Christ. The only distinctive exception is Jesus Christ, who is not created, but who is the unique and distinct One who is symmetric to humanity by virtue of his incarnated humanity, but asymmetrically distinct with regard to his complete divinity; the unity of his divine-human ontology redeems us, re-equalizes our relationships when in our sinfulness and waywardness we subjugate, oppress, or delegitimize our fellow human beings by diminishing someone's humanity, limiting the exercise of someone's gifts, or discouraging someone's desire to serve Jesus Christ and the body of believers because of the same desire to limit and diminish. To be faithful to the Scriptures, the overall thrust and content the Scriptures and the gospel witness, is to follow the tact of Paul in 1 Corinthians and 1 Timothy and to pastorally exhort the community to hold one another accountable when there is unhelpful disruption, usurpation of authority, and overly passionate people (men and women alike) who are getting on their high horses and not teaching the gospel or teaching in ways that they have an air of a know-it-all. Call the assembly to account when individuals or groups are doing things that bring attention more to themselves (perhaps by the volume and velocity of their advocacy, the volume and velocity of their particular theological and ecclesiastical platforms and agenda, or maybe because of how they dress—flaunting their material blessings and so becoming a stumbling block to those who don't have as much; in a case like this, the ostentation of a few obscures the call to the whole church to be in solidarity with the marginalized, with the hungry, and with the thirsty.

Far from silencing God's people, the Lord has always been about proclaiming God's truth, God's praises, and God's love. This is not to say that silence is never called for. Of course, moments and seasons of silence are necessary; silence is an essential aspect of maturing faith, a way of following what the Psalms indicate in the annotated rubric "Selah." We need Selah to pause, to reflect, to meditate, and to pray. Even Jesus Christ our Lord retreated after feeding the thousands and healing the many in order to pray and reflect, and even when he rejoiced with his friends in the boat, he took a nap during the storm. So, we are called to be still and know that God is God (Ps 46:10). Jesus also silenced his disciples when they were about to make a hasty judgment and send away hungry crowds (Matt 14:13–21; 15:32–39; Mark 6:30–44; 8:1–10; Luke 9:10–17), when they were ready to send away a mother pleading for her daughter's healing (Matt 15:21–28; Mark 7:24–30), and when they saw children as irritants (Matt 19:13–15; Mark 10:13–16; Luke 18:15–16). Why did Jesus silence the disciples? Because their silence and muteness meant death to the hungry crowds, despair and death to the pleading mother and struggling daughter, and sadness to expectant children and parents. Whereas the disciples remained silent in the face of needy people, Jesus spoke to them. The God of Israel and of Jesus is the living God (in contrast to idols) precisely because God speaks. Jesus spoke, and God speaks because God is the living God, because God is the living God: the living God speaks (cf. Ps 135:15–17; Hab 2:18–20) In the times that the Lord directs silence, it is in the silence that God's people receive instruction and have opportunity to heed God's word and to reflect upon it. And then there is a time to proclaim, preach, teach, and live what you and I have seen and heard.

Far from silencing and delegitimizing half the human population, half of a congregation, the Scriptures and the Lord of the Scriptures seeks freedom for creation, freedom from sin, freedom from bondage and captivity to the self-destructive powers and principalities that subjugate, oppress, and prevent us from living into the life and love of God in Jesus Christ through the Spirit. How discouraging, enervating, and death-dealing it is for religious authorities, for religious bodies, and for the policies and confessional statements of those same religious bodies who praise the name of Jesus Christ—who should be living in the freedom of the resurrection light—to suppress women from living into their callings to serve Jesus Christ as church leaders! Rather, the redemptive, salvific work of God in Jesus Christ through the Holy Spirit, as attested to us by the sacred Scriptures of the Old and New Testaments, has restored us to be a new creation, where all people are equal in the sight of God and with one another, and are called to bear witness to that freedom in Christ. Such good news cannot and should not be contained. Otherwise, God would even call and move upon the dead stones to shout if need be!

NOW WHAT?

As I have chronicled above, my questioning of the biblical and theological approaches of the conservative wing of the Reformed theological tradition occurred prior to my experiencing the faithful preaching of women ministers and the astute leadership of women pastors, seminary professors, and executive church leaders. Mine was not a case of experience changing my biblical and theological interpretation; it was my questioning and examination of the Scriptures and of Reformed theology that led me to see women in church leadership in a new, redemptive way that had been obscured by the conservative theological approach of Westminster Seminary California.

What are some tangible ways I have tried to be a consistent male coconspirator?[4] Since my ordination to the ministry of Word and Sacrament in 2003, and (prior to that) during my involvement in the Presbyterian Church (U.S.A.)'s General Assembly Council, the Lord has opened up multiple and diverse opportunities in education, ministry service, and community service to exercise leadership and advocacy for my sisters in the faith and to support them in their vocational calling and professional empowerment. This gender study guide is the capstone of a three-year Collaborative Inquiry Team project grant from the Louisville Institute where I have served as one of two men coconspirators on an initiative that has sought to analyze the intersectional forces in Asian American and Latinx churches in Southern California that either support or stifle women in the ordered ministries of the church. In my current role as Board chair of the Presbyterian Foundation, the fiduciary of the Presbyterian Church (U.S.A.) with about $2 billion in assets under management and $73 million in annual disbursements to support mission and ministries in the US and around the world, I am focusing on diversity, equity, and inclusion as one of three main priorities during my two-year term as Board chair to insure that the culture, ethos, and policies of the Foundation's Board and staff—and especially the senior management team—cultivate and support women of color in key leadership positions, and with that, a dignifying of cultural and perspectival diversity as it relates to socioeconomic contexts, theological and political lenses, and life experiences. At the adjournment of the historic 224th General Assembly of the Presbyterian Church (U.S.A.) held via Zoom in 2020, I teamed up with my fellow Moderators, Co-Moderators, and Vice Moderators of prior General Assemblies as one of the principal coauthors of a major churchwide statement that named the specific ways

4. I am indebted to my friend and colleague the Reverend Laura Mariko Cheifetz, assistant dean of vocation at Vanderbilt Divinity School, for the term *coconspirator*. She averred that to be a coconspirator is more than being an ally. A coconspirator engages deeply and faithfully in the struggle, putting oneself on the line, supporting others in the struggle for justice, and conspiring ways to transform aspiration into action.

the Assembly failed to support Black women and girls specifically, and communities of color generally, and offered constructive ways in which we could support and resource the Assembly in order not repeat those failures in our structural and ecclesial life that privileges whiteness. I recently joined several of my Filipino American scholar colleagues in procuring a grant from the Louisville Institute to analyze Filipino American theology (two-thirds of our team being Filipina women) as we look at intersectional factors in communal identity formation for Filipino American communities in a time of pandemic. At the invitation of Korean American clergy-women, I offered the foreword for an edited volume that lifts up the voices and experiences of my siblings in the faith whose perspectives have often been silenced by the patriarchal leadership of Korean and Korean American churches. I have been a panelist at an annual Racial Ethnic Seminarians Conference organized by the Presbyterian Mission Agency to provide support, guidance, and practical assistance for communities of color as they discerned their call to ministry. Through my work in the World Alliance of Reformed Churches and the World Communion of Reformed Churches, I have worked alongside colleagues from different continents in advocating for gender justice in the conciliar structures of Reformed churches, lifting up healthy models of masculinity over and against oppressive contexts and ideologies that diminish the humanity of women and girls. And as noted previously, when I was given the chance, I exercised the full prerogative as outgoing Moderator of the 220th General Assembly (between 2012 and 2014) to appoint persons of color, mostly women of color—including an Asian American and a Puerto Rican—for the six vacancies that I was privileged to fill, and with the intentionality of tilting the majority of the General Assembly Nominating Committee to persons of color. And while there was some question from church executives as to what I was doing, I gave my reasons, was respected for it, and proceeded to make the appointments. More recently, in the aftermath of George Floyd's death on May 25, 2020, I joined about forty other AAPI church leaders to organize a solidarity prayer vigil with Black leaders and Black churches in Southern California. There is ongoing work, to be sure, but the planning, the actual event, and the post-event work has supported and lifted up the voices of my AAPI sisters, as we together name the ways in which the AAPI community has been complicit and complacent in addressing and engaging racial inequality and racial inequity.

In short, as a male Filipino American coconspirator, I am committed to the long, arduous journey for racial justice and gender justice. With respect to my Asian American and Latinx sisters in the faith and in ministry, it is my prayerful hope that the day comes when every one of the Christian theological traditions will affirm and support Asian American and Latinx women in the ordered ministries of the church, and will support them to serve in every part of the church. Such support will enable the church of Jesus Christ to include all parts of the body of Christ in being sent to live and proclaim good news (apostolicity), to affirm the diversity of giftedness that God has called for the purpose of gospel work (catholicity), to support the sacredness of our individual and collective calling (holiness), and to underscore that every part of the body of Christ matters (oneness/unity). May it be so!

IMPLICATIONS FOR TODAY'S PULPIT

As we seek concrete action to effect gender justice in our churches, an important and principal place where that occurs and must occur is at the pulpit. It is from the pulpit, through consistent and constant commitment to preach the transformative Word to the people of God that we find that radical change happens.

Gender justice from the pulpit requires the confluence of the community/congregation context, the perspectival and interpretive approach to scriptural texts, and the subtexts of the preacher's own wrestling with Scripture, context, and their own personal theological, cultural, emotional, psychological, and spiritual commitments and struggles. The sermons that are preached, the Bible studies that are taught, and the embodiment of the message with the preacher/teacher's incarnational presence are essential elements in how the Spirit of God transforms individuals and whole communities.

Here are some questions to reflect upon with respect to scriptural texts, the context, and the subtext:

Implications for Today's Pulpit:
On the Text of Scripture:

1. How do you understand 1 Cor 14:33–36 and 1 Tim 2:11–14?

2. What was the immediate context of those texts in the first century CE?

3. How do those texts connect with the larger agenda of the New Testament and with the overall salvific vision of God in terms of the reconciliation of the entirety of humanity and of all creation?

4. What do commentaries from a wide theological spectrum say about these texts? What are the gaps in those commentaries?

Implications for Today's Pulpit:
On the Context of the Congregation or Worshiping Community

1. What other obstacles (e.g., theological or ecclesiastical rules, processes, or gender-specific resources) beyond biblical interpretation and application of these scriptural texts prevent women being fully recognized, welcomed, authorized, legitimized, and supported in their callings to serve in senior pastoral leadership in your congregational or ministry context?

2. What is your congregation's or worshipping community's commitment—both stated and unstated, both spoken and as actually practiced—to gender equality and gender equity for women in church leadership?

3. How does your congregation or worshiping community understand their calling in their particularity, and how can sermons on gender justice challenge or strengthen the mission, vision, and values of this congregation or worshiping community?

4. What are the fears of your congregation or worshiping community about their communal life and about their sense of being a part of God's future? What hopes do they have about God's future? Do they see women in church leadership and women leading as part and essential to God's present future? If not, why not?

5. What items for confession does your congregation or worshiping community need to include in their communal prayer of confession each week with respect to gender equality and gender equity?

Implications for Today's Pulpit:
On the Subtext of the Preacher or Teacher

1. What are the contexts that you grew up in, that you have served, and that you are serving? Have those situational contexts limited or expanded your understanding of God, of the Scripture, of who you are, and of your vocational calling?

2. What fears and joys do you have in preaching and teaching specifically from 1 Cor 14:33–36 and 1 Tim 2:11–14?

3. How do you understand your ministry vocation with respect to gender equality and gender equity in church and in society?

4. What word of confession do you need to say in the communal prayer of confession each week with respect to gender equality and gender equity in the church and in society?

BIBLIOGRAPHY

Bradshaw, Paul F., et al. *The Apostolic Tradition: A Commentary*. Hermeneia. Minneapolis: Fortress, 2002.

Cortez, Felix H. "The Argument of the Order of Creation in 1 Timothy 2:9–15." *Andrews University Faculty Publications* (February 2013) Paper 13. https://digitalcommons. andrews.edu/cgi/viewcontent.cgi?article=1012&context=new-testament-pubs/.

Macy, Gary. *The Hidden History of Women's Ordination: Female Clergy in the Medieval West*. Oxford: Oxford University Press, 2008.